ROBIN HOOD

THE LIFE AND LEGEND OF AN OUTLAW

D0556210

Dedicated to Joseph and Deborah Basdeo, and my cat, Robin, named after Robin Hood.

ROBIN HOOD
THE LIFE AND LEGEND
OF AN OUTLAW

Stephen Basdeo

PEN & SWORD
HISTORY

AN IMPRINT OF PEN & SWORD BOOKS LTD.
YORKSHIRE – PHILADELPHIA

First published in Great Britain in 2019 by
PEN AND SWORD HISTORY
an imprint of
Pen and Sword Books Ltd
Yorkshire - Philadelphia

Hardback ISBN 978 1 52672 981 1
Paperback ISBN 978 1 52675 758 6

Typeset in Times New Roman 11/13.5 by
Aura Technology and Software Services, India

Printed and bound in the UK by TJ International

Pen & Sword Books Ltd incorporates the imprints of Pen & Sword
Archaeology, Atlas, Aviation, Battleground, Discovery,
Family History, History, Maritime, Military, Naval, Politics, Railways,
Select, Social History, Transport, True Crime, Claymore Press,
Frontline Books, Leo Cooper, Praetorian Press, Remember When,
Seaforth Publishing and Wharncliffe.

For a complete list of Pen & Sword titles please contact
PEN & SWORD BOOKS LIMITED
47 Church Street, Barnsley, South Yorkshire, S70 2AS, England
E-mail: enquiries@pen-and-sword.co.uk
Website: www.pen-and-sword.co.uk

or

PEN AND SWORD BOOKS
1950 Lawrence Rd, Havertown, PA 19083, USA
E-mail: uspen-and-sword@casematepublishers.com
Website: www.penandswordbooks.com

Contents

Acknowledgements

There are always too many people to thank in this section of a book. First and foremost I would like to thank my former supervisors who are the best mentors any aspiring graduate student could hope to have, Professor Paul Hardwick, Professor Rosemary Mitchell, and Dr Alaric Hall. I thank you for guiding me through my PhD and helping to develop my skills as a historian. And Paul, I think that I have remembered to say 'the text says' instead of 'the text said'. I still can't quite get the hang of it but if you see me falling into my old ways, don't judge! (Hopefully these will have been ironed out by the editor anyway!) Special mention always goes to my family: Debbie and Joseph Basdeo, Jamila Garrod, her husband Ped, and my two nieces, Mya and Alexa. And of course to the three men in my life: Richard Neesam, Chris Williams, and Sam Dowling.

Obviously, the constraints of writing a popular history book mean that I get very little space to include footnotes and citations to relevant secondary sources. However, it would be criminal of me not to give some brief mentions to fellow scholars whose work has helped, informed, and inspired me in writing this book. First there is my good friend, Allen Wright. His website was very useful to me when I was a young graduate student cobbling together a doctoral research proposal on Robin Hood, and I still find his site an excellent and trustworthy place for when I need to quickly check a fact.

Special thanks must go to Professor Alexander Kaufman and Dr Valerie Johnson. I met them in 2015 at the Robin Hood Studies conference, and since then, although they work in the USA, they have given me a lot of positive feedback and constructive criticism on various Robin Hood articles and website posts I have written. The help I have received from them over the years has enhanced my own knowledge of Robin Hood and of course helped me to develop my own profile as a researcher.

Dr Lesley Coote was the external examiner for my PhD entitled 'The Changing Faces of Robin Hood, c. 1700–c. 1900'. To Lesley I say thank you

ACKNOWLEDGEMENTS

for not only being my external examiner but also giving me the opportunity to speak at the Robin Hood conference and the panels at various other conferences. And of course to Dr Mark Truesdale, with whom I've spent time at conferences and via email talking about all things Robin Hood! And no, Mark, there was no way in hell that I would even consider including in this book a discussion of the horrendous Robin Hood kung-fu movie, *Robin Hood, Arrows, Beans, and Karate*, that we watched in a drunken haze the evening before the Medieval Congress in Leeds in 2017. Some things are best left in the archive!

There are several researchers whom I have never met but whose work has informed both my PhD research and this book. Such people include Stephen Knight, Thomas Hahn (with whom I have had a few brief email exchanges over the past couple of years), Thomas Ohlgren, Graham Seal, even if I do disagree with them upon some points on Robin Hood related things. Where these researchers have raised specific points they are always credited by name in the text. Special thanks, of course, goes to the lovely people at Pen and Sword Books for commissioning me to write this one. Jon Wright and Laura Hirst have been wonderful, putting up with many proof changes and edits. And thank you to my editor, Karyn Burnham, for constructive feedback on this manuscript.

I would like to point out here that all of the images in this book are from antiquarian and first edition works in my personal collection, and there are, therefore, no museums or galleries to thank at this time. Such is the absurdity of current licensing rules and regulations that it is often cheaper for authors to spend around £20 or £30 on an old eighteenth- or nineteenth-century book or print containing the out-of-copyright images that you need, rather than pay excessive licensing fees from museums and archives. To use just one image, a friend of mine was quoted £200 recently. Surely this cannot be right? It amounts to a tax paid by researchers upon the dissemination of knowledge. And no, the publishers themselves cannot reimburse authors for these drastically high costs due to their own publishing costs. If they did, it would mean that publishers would not be as willing to take chances on books such as this, which are outside of the usual Tudors and World War Two popular history repertoire. In a book about Robin Hood, who is said to have fought against unjust taxes and costs, the brunt of which was felt by the common people, I felt it fitting that I at least air.

Introduction

The merry pranks he playd, would ask an age to tell,
And the aduentures strange that Robin Hood befell,
When Mansfield many a time for Robin hath bin layd,
How he hath cosned them, that him would have betrayd;
How often he hath come to Nottingham disguisd,
And cunningly escapt, being set to be surprizd.
In this our spacious Isle, I thinke there is not one,
But he hath heard some talke of him and little Iohn;
And to the end of time, the Tales shall ne'r be done,
Of Scarlock, George a Greene, and Much the Millers sonne,
Of Tuck the merry Frier, which many a Sermon made,
In praise of Robin Hood, his Out-lawes, and their Trade.

Michael Drayton, *Poly-Olbion* (1612–22)

The adventurous life of the gallant outlaw, Robin Hood, has long been a favourite theme of song and story in England. True, the historian must often ask in vain for documents verifying the wild doings of the famous robber. But there is a mass of legend referring to our Hero which bears the seal of genuineness upon its face and throws a flood of light on the manners and customs of his epoch.

Alexandre Dumas, *The Prince of Thieves* (1863)

Since at least the fourteenth century, Robin Hood has occupied an important place in English popular culture; he is the quintessential noble robber who lives in the forest and steals from the rich and gives to the poor. His true love is Maid Marian. His most trusted friend and fellow outlaw is Little John. His lieutenants, Will Scarlet, Allen-a-Dale, and Friar Tuck, are fellow robbers who help him outwit the dastardly schemes of the Sheriff of Nottingham. Drayton's words, cited above, are as true today as they were at the time he was writing: Robin Hood is indeed one of the most famous legendary English figures. Throughout the centuries in poems, ballads, plays, novels, and films, the outlaw's story has been reimagined and reinterpreted by various authors. As a legend that has hitherto proved itself to be infinitely adaptable, it is likely that we will see Robin Hood on the big and small screen, and in books, for many years to come. This book is the story of how the legend of Robin Hood has been continually reshaped over time in British popular culture by different authors, in a variety of different contexts, and for varying audiences.

However, the first thing that readers often ask, and which should be settled in any book about Robin Hood, is whether he was a real person or not. Many historians, both professional and amateur, have endeavoured to identify a historical outlaw in medieval court records whose life may have given rise to the many stories that now exist about Robin Hood. The truth is, however, that no one will ever be sure if they have found 'the one', so to speak. As my friend Allen Wright, a Robin Hood scholar based in Canada, has often been fond of saying: 'no one is ever sure who the real Robin Hood is, unless they have a book to sell: then they are sure.' My personal view is in agreement with Professor James C. Holt, who holds that one of the men named as Robin Hood in court rolls during the 1220s, from Yorkshire, is *most likely* to be the real Robin Hood. Of course, we can never know this for sure. I hesitate to agree with Professor Stephen Knight who would reduce Robin Hood to being a literary creation, and who thinks it is a mythic name; for Knight, a person became Robin Hood if they went shooting deer in the forest, much like a person becomes Father Christmas if they give out presents at Christmas time.

Yet throughout the centuries, Robin Hood was always assumed to have been a historical figure, by medieval chroniclers, early modern antiquaries, and Victorian and modern historians. In fact, it is only recently that Robin Hood's historicity – the idea of him having been an actual person – has seriously been called into question, especially since Robin Hood studies took what scholars call a 'literary turn'. Since the 1990s, Robin Hood scholars in the field of literary studies have turned away from archival research and the search for a real Robin Hood in order to concentrate their studies on the content and context of the early Robin Hood poems. While I understand Knight's reasoning, the fact that we find a man named Robin

Hood who was listed as an outlaw, or fugitive, in court rolls, as well as the fact that the name of Robin Hood was used as an alias by later medieval criminals, suggests that there must be a grain of truth to the idea of an historical outlaw. It is very hard for ideas to emerge from nothing at all. The Father Christmas analogy was perhaps the wrong one to make anyway, for we know that our modern idea of Father Christmas, or Santa Claus for American readers, is based in part on the historical figure of Saint Nicholas of Myra (270–343). Even a thief who is seemingly as fictional as Charles Dickens's Fagin in *Oliver Twist* (1838) had some basis in reality: a few years before Dickens set pen to paper to write his masterpiece, the trial of a Jewish fence named Isaac 'Ikey' Solomon (c. 1787–1850) caused a sensation in London, and there are many similarities between Ikey's trial reports and the trial of Fagin related in the fifty-second chapter of Dickens's novel. Perhaps those who have studied the crimes of Jack the Ripper will also understand: we know for a fact that murders occurred in Whitechapel, London, in 1888, and that they must have been perpetrated by someone whose crimes have been subsequently ascribed to Jack the Ripper. Historians do not, however, know who that person is. And just for the record, as both a medievalist and a crime historian, I would like to point out that just as no one has ever been able to *definitively* prove who the real Robin Hood was, so no one has ever been able to successfully identify the perpetrator of the Ripper crimes, in spite of the number of books claiming otherwise.

However, let us briefly consider some of the likely candidates who could have been the real Robin Hood. Most people are familiar with modern portrayals of Robin Hood being set during the time of 'bad' King John, or perhaps a little earlier in the days of 'good' King Richard. Medieval Robin Hood poems did not place the outlaw during this time, however, but in the period of an unspecified king named Edward. It was not until the seventeenth century that scholars began to make a serious effort to locate a real Robin Hood in court records, and even then, most of those writing about Robin Hood in that century often simply invented facts, as we see in some of the 'histories' of Robin Hood published in that period. The first major breakthrough came in 1852, when an antiquary named Joseph Hunter, who worked in the Public Record Office, identified a man named Robyn Hood in records from the 1320s who not only lived in the time of a king named Edward, in this case Edward II, but whose life appeared to corroborate the events described in the longest and most significant of the three surviving medieval Robin Hood poems entitled *A Gest of Robyn Hode*. Although we will learn more about this poem in the coming chapters, it is worth mentioning a few details about it here. Towards the end of the story, King Edward travels into the forest in disguise and meets Robin Hood. The men share a meal and participate in a good-natured archery competition. After this, the king reveals his identity to the outlaws and Robin is pardoned. Robin is then invited to serve the king in his court. However, Robin only stays in the king's service for just over a year before returning to the greenwood. The details found by Hunter of the life of the man named Robyn Hood seem to correlate with the events related in the *Gest*. This Robyn Hood served as a porter to the king between March and November 1324, after which he was paid off for being infirm. So far so good – this Robyn's time spent as a servant to the king was not quite the 'twelve monethes and three' which the *Gest* says Robin spent in service, but it was close enough. Hunter's find gained even more credibility when he connected the Robyn Hood who was servant to the king to a man called Robert Hood, who was recorded as having lived in Wakefield between 1316 and 1317. What made this Robert Hood of Wakefield particularly noteworthy is the fact that he was married to a woman named Matilda, and in an influential sixteenth-century play by Anthony Munday, Robin Hood's wife is named Matilda before adopting the name of Maid Marian. However, scholars know now that the character of Maid Marian has no basis in any historical figure. Another aspect of Hunter's discovery which seemed to lend it credibility, however, is the fact that his Robert Hood lived in Wakefield. The Yorkshire town of Wakefield is, of course, not too far from Barnsdale, which is where Robin Hood's activities are located in the *Gest*. It truly seemed as though Hunter had cracked the case, even if there was no piece of evidence explicitly stating that this Robert Hood was an outlaw.

As we will see in the next chapter, however, it is not wise to assume that the events that are related in that early Robin Hood poem are historical facts because the *Gest* itself incorporates many contemporary tropes found in other texts, notably the 'king and commoner' tradition, recently studied in depth by Mark Truesdale. These types of tales usually feature a king venturing in disguise into a rural area of England and meeting and sharing a meal with a peasant. The commoner rails against the injustices perpetrated by local officials such as sheriffs and abbots, often perpetrated in the king's name. After the meal the king then reveals his identity and invites the commoner to his court and gives him a reward. These stories of kings meeting their subjects often rivalled stories of Robin Hood in their popularity. As for the king being named in the *Gest*,

Truesdale says, it is also possible that the king in the *Gest* was called Edward just because it was a name which sounded royal, much like Henry. These considerations did not occur to Hunter and presumably, the fact that Hunter's Robin Hood was alive in the 1320s would have given enough time for stories about his life to emerge and circulate so that, by c. 1377, William Langland could reference 'rymes of Robyn Hode' in his poem *Piers Plowman*.

As a result of further research, more people called Robin Hood were found in medieval court records. The only explanation for this is that Robin Hood's fame and notoriety was so great that other criminals began using the name as an alias. In Norfolk in 1441, a group of revellers blocked the road and threatened to murder a local magnate named Sir Geoffrey Harsyk. By all accounts they continually chanted 'We are Robynhodesmen, war war war!' In 1498, a man named Roger Marshall led a gang of nearly 100 men to a village fair in Staffordshire and caused a riot. At his court hearing, he called himself Robin Hood.

Hunter's fourteenth-century Robert Hood discovery evidently did not fit with the traditional dating of the Robin Hood legend, which sees the outlaw and his men active in the 1190s and early 1200s, during the reigns of King Richard I and King John. It was the Scottish chronicler, John Major, who, writing in *Historia Maioris Britanniae* (1521), originally placed Robin Hood in this time period. From Major's time through to the early twentieth century, the reigns of Richard and John were assumed to have been the period in which Robin Hood flourished, even if the theory was not supported by documentary records. There was a man who appropriated the name of Robert Hood who, in 1216, killed Ralph of Cirencester in the local abbot's garden, but historians have dismissed this figure because it is too far away from either Yorkshire or Nottinghamshire. Thus, it was Hunter's discoveries and theories that seemed to make sense, at least until the 1930s when L. V. D. Owen found a reference to a man named Robert Hod in the Yorkshire Assize records for 1225–26 (called Hobbehod in some of the accounts for later years). This Robert was listed as 'fugitive' and began to seem like a worthier candidate for a historical outlaw than the man of the 1320s, especially in view of the fact that he was a fugitive because he was in debt to the Liberty of St Peter's in York, which would have made him a tenant of the Archbishop of York. And in *A Gest of Robyn Hode*, one of Robin's arch-enemies is the Abbot of York. During the 1980s, David Crook argued that this Robert Hod, fugitive, was the same man as

INTRODUCTION

Robert of Wetherby, who was listed as an 'outlaw and evil-doer of our land' in the same decade, although he did not provide any particularly compelling evidence to connect Robert Hod with Robert of Wetherby. Although Robert Hod was listed as an outlaw, in fact, there is no firm evidence to suggest that he was a bandit of the type depicted in the *Gest*. However, further facts seemed to be falling into place: it just so happened that the man who was charged with hunting down this Robert of Wetherby was a man named Eustace of Lowdham, the High Sheriff of York. Prior to taking up his appointment at York, however, Lowdham was the High Sheriff of Nottingham. Thus, this Robert Hod/Robert of Wetherby could have been *the* Robin Hood. As we will see shortly in the succeeding chapter, this would also explain why, in late-medieval Robin Hood poems, Robin Hood, although based in Barnsdale, Yorkshire, was pursued by 'the hye sheryfe of Notynghame'. This vague biography which seemed to be emerging of this Robert Hod's life seemed to make sense with the reputed date of Robin's death in 1247. That date was allegedly inscribed on a grave-stone in Kirklees, as recorded in the private papers by Thomas Gale, Dean of York, in 1702. This Robert Hod of Wetherby's life, then, seemed to follow these circumstances: he was active as an outlaw in the 1190s, as recorded by certain chroniclers; he was still an outlaw in 1225 when he appears in the assize records; during this time he was pursued by the Sheriff of York and had died by 1247. His notoriety would then have been sufficient for his life story to acquire semi-legendary status by c. 1262, when a man named William, who had been outlawed, assumed the alias of William Robehod.

Obviously many Yorkshire place names have been mentioned thus far. Nottinghamshire and Sherwood have been favoured as the location for Robin Hood's old stomping grounds in many twentieth-century portrayals of the Robin Hood legend. Only two of the earliest Robin Hood texts, *Robin Hood and the Monk* (c. 1465), and *Robin Hood and the Potter* (c. 1468), clearly place Robin in Nottingham. Otherwise, there has historically been a strong connection between Yorkshire and the Robin Hood legend, Drayton's words above notwithstanding. Andrew of Wyntoun's *Orygynale Chronicle* (c. 1420) says, for example, that,

Litil Iohun and Robert Hude	*Little John and Robin Hood*
Waythmen war commendit gud;	*Outlaws were commended good.*
In Ingilwode and Bernnysdaile	*In Inglewood and Barnsdale*
Þai oyssit al þis tyme þar trawale.	*They practised their labour.*

Later chronicles such as Walter Bower's continuation of John of Fordun's *Scotichronicon* (c. 1440) similarly place the site of Robin Hood and Little John's exploits in the forest of Barnsdale, Yorkshire. Richard Grafton's *Chronicle at Large* (1569), whose information is based upon 'an olde and auncient pamphlet' (which was probably *A Gest of Robyn Hode*) also situates the outlaw's band in Yorkshire. Grafton's account is also the first to imply that Robin Hood was either born, or in the latter part of his life became, an earl. We do not see Robin formally styled as the famous Earl of Huntingdon, however, until two plays written by Anthony Munday entitled *The Downfall of Robert, Earl of Huntington* and *The Death of Robert, Earl of Huntingdon* (1597–98). In these plays, the sites of Robin's activities range throughout both Nottingham and Yorkshire:

> *Scar.* Its ful seauen yeares since we were outlawed first,
> And wealthy Sherwood was our heritage:
> For all those yeares we rainged uncontrolde,
> From Barnsdale shrogs to Notinghams red cliffs,
> At Blithe and Tickhill we were welcome guests.
> Good George a Greene at Bradford was our friend,
> And wanton Wakefields pinner lou'd as well.
> At Barnsley dwels a Potter tough and strong,
> That neuer brookt, we brethren should haue wrong.
> The Nunnes of Farnsfield, pretty nunnes they bee,
> Gaue napkins, shirts, and bands to him and mee.
> Bateman of Kendall, gaue us Kendall greene,
> And Sharpe of Leedes, sharp arrows for us made:
> At Rotherham dwelt our bowyer, God him blisse,
> Iackson he hight, his bowes did neuer misse.

Even during the early modern period there was clearly debate about the region in which Robin Hood was said to have flourished. The connection between Robin Hood and Nottinghamshire was only firmly established in popular culture at quite a late point in the development of the legend, and stories of Robin Hood were still being set in Barnsdale, Yorkshire, even into the nineteenth century. This is why many historians in the past have sought to find a real Robin Hood in Yorkshire and not in Nottinghamshire.

It should be noted that the many place names and landmarks associated with Robin Hood in Yorkshire have a tenuous link to the legend at best. Landmarks erected in the past which purported to be where Robin Hood slept or where he stopped for a drink are mostly early modern in origin without any links to either the historical Robin Hoods mentioned above or the early poems. There is Robin Hood's cave, near Ollerton, a town fairly close to Sherwood Forest; Robin Hood's well is in Skellow, near Barnsley, and in the eighteenth century this landmark was, in the spirit of Robin Hood, a place where paupers begged for alms, as recorded by Thomas Gent in *The History of York* (1730):

> Over a spring call'd Robin Hoods Well ... is a very handsome stone arch, erected by the Lord Carlisle, where passengers from the coach frequently drink of the fair water, and give their charity to two people who attend there.

There is also a grave in Hathersage, Lincolnshire, which purports to be the place where Little John was buried. The most famous Yorkshire landmark with connections to Robin Hood is the gatehouse of Kirklees Priory. Out of the window of the upper story of this small building is the place from which Robin is said to have shot his last arrow. A short distance away from there is Robin Hood's grave, which does not date from the medieval period but is an early modern construction. Some local amateur historians have attempted to identify the Prioress of Kirklees, the woman whom, as we shall see, killed Robin Hood. These researchers have found a likely suspect in the person of Elizabeth De Staynton, who served as prioress between 1331 and 1347. In view of the fact that the most likely historical outlaw is the Robin Hood of the 1220s, however, it is highly unlikely that De Staynton had anything to do with Robin Hood.

Of course, tentative language has been used in this short introduction. Robert Hod of the 1220s *could* have been the historical outlaw whose life and deeds gave rise to the legend. And the most enthusiastic proponent of the candidate from the 1220s, James C. Holt, admitted that 'believing' this Robin Hood was the historical outlaw required much faith.

When scholars are dealing with medieval marginalia and one or two references to men named Robin Hood in court rolls, it is unlikely that we will ever be able to prove beyond reasonable doubt that Robert Hod of Wetherby was the real Robin Hood. Thus, perhaps the best attitude to take towards the study of the real Robin Hood is the following given by Alexander Kaufman: 'the origins of Robin Hood the person and his original context are perhaps best left to those individuals who wish to search for that which is forever to be a quest'.

Aside from archival research, some utterly bizarre theories of Robin Hood's origins were posited by nineteenth-century historians. Thomas

Wright in the Victorian period equated the outlaw with a Teutonic forest spirit named Hudekin. Amazingly, there are plenty of books written by modern-day folklorists which still support the idea of Robin Hood as a forest elf/spirit. Some have even attempted to argue that the name of Robin Hood is the product of orgies which apparently occurred in England's woodlands in some far off point in time, a claim which appeared from one writer in the *Guardian* in 2010. These claims are usually made without a shred of evidence to support them. This book does not enter into detail upon these quite frankly absurd ideas which were discredited at the moment of their inception in the nineteenth century, again by P. Valentine Harris in the 1950s.

Whoever he may have been, it is Robin Hood's legend that ultimately forms a more interesting basis for study. Through studying the changing portrayals of Robin Hood from the medieval to the modern periods, we can learn, not just about Robin Hood, as interesting as that is for its own sake, but also about the society from which those stories emerged. This is because no artistic or literary work can ever be fully understood when viewed independently from its author or contemporary political, social, and cultural context. Thus, we will not only study the various Robin Hood texts and films that have been produced throughout the ages, but we will also ask why they were written. This book does not ask whether this or that portrayal of Robin Hood and the medieval period was 'historically accurate' or not, unless a certain depiction of Robin Hood is blatantly and amusingly riddled with factual errors, such as in *Robin Hood: Prince of Thieves* (1991) or the ghastly *New Adventures of Robin Hood* (1997). The authors of various periods who wrote books about Robin Hood rarely made an attempt to be so accurate. In any case, it is from these often inaccurate portrayals of the medieval past that our modern conceptions of Robin Hood have been constructed. The Robin Hood we know today is an amalgamation of many different stories. As we will see, we owe our understanding of Robin Hood as not only an outlaw, but also a freedom fighter, to eighteenth and nineteenth-century portrayals of him.

It should be noted at this point that I present a chronological overview of the legend of Robin Hood. While some readers may have preferred this study of Robin Hood texts to be arranged by themes or genres, because stories of Robin Hood did not emerge over time in a uniform way, but were disparate and subject to variation, this should be reflected in any history of Robin Hood. At one point, ballads might simultaneously be popular with plays or prose texts. In the Victorian period, novels were clearly the most popular form for disseminating the Robin Hood story. Presenting the history of the Robin Hood legend in such a way will give readers an insight into its uneven development. The only exception to this chronological approach is where an examination of certain texts in strict chronological order would lead to unnecessary repetition. This will be the case with discussions of early modern ballads; three are discussed in detail as being representative of the types of stories that were circulating during the seventeenth century, but others are referred to and discussed at other points, notably in places where novelists and filmmakers drew upon material from them.

This book is, of course, a study of Robin Hood in British popular culture. Deciding what was truly popular was, at times, a difficult task. Obviously famous texts such as *A Gest of Robyn Hode*, and the works of famous authors and poets, such as Walter Scott and John Keats, are discussed in this book, as well as twentieth-century films. Early modern ballads must also appear in any discussion of Robin Hood in popular culture. Some works, however, were not popular, inasmuch as they did not reach a wide audience, but they did have a profound influence upon successive portrayals of Robin Hood. We will see this when we examine Anthony Munday's plays, *The Downfall of Robert, Earle of Huntington* and *The Death of Robert, Earle of Huntingdon* (1597–98). They were influential inasmuch as they were the first artistic works to depict Robin Hood as an aristocrat who had lost his lands and was subsequently outlawed, but the actual plays were performed once and only to a small audience. Other stories that have been influenced by tales of Robin Hood must also be considered, such as Robert Louis Stevenson's *The Black Arrow* (1888) and, in our own century, of course, we have the television series, *Arrow*, which is based upon the Green Arrow series of comics.

Yet this is not just a book about Robin Hood books and films, as interesting as a study of them often is because another part of popular culture in the nineteenth and early twentieth centuries were Empire Day pageants. At these events, children were encouraged to dress up as figures from English history, and Robin Hood was a popular one with children and adults alike. Dressing up as Robin Hood, in fact, was not a pastime limited to late-Victorian children; earlier in the Victorian period, adults at the Eglington Tournament dressed as characters from *Ivanhoe*.

The first and second chapters examine stories of Robin Hood that can be dated with some precision to the late-medieval period. At this point in time, poems circulated by word of mouth. Many Robin Hood poems have undoubtedly been lost to history but luckily, thanks to some individuals who wrote them down in the fifteenth century, we have the text of three early poems: *Robin Hood and the Monk*, *Robin Hood and the Potter*, and *A Gest of Robyn Hode*. These tales were enjoyed predominantly by town-dwelling and relatively affluent listeners, but Robin Hood would also have been encountered by people in more humble stations of life in the many Robin Hood village games which were held in rural areas during the medieval and early modern period, and a little later than this we have accounts of King Henry VIII playing Robin Hood, and records of village games in the late-medieval period.

The third chapter continues our journey through history into a period which scholars call 'early modern'. Varying dates have been given as starting points and end points for this era, which is to be expected when historians are attempting to generalise. In this book, early modern means the period of time stretching from the sixteenth to the eighteenth century. This is truly a transformative era in the legend: Robin Hood began to be depicted in plays and ballads as a dispossessed nobleman. What is surprising about many early modern portrayals of Robin Hood is the fact that, especially in ballads, he is depicted as a rather inept and ineffective outlaw. In some texts, such as Ben Jonson's *The Sad Shepherd* (1641), it is unclear whether Robin Hood is a thief at all.

Portrayals of Robin Hood are always hard to categorise neatly. We see patriotic portrayals of Robin Hood discussed in the fourth chapter, which examines plays from the eighteenth century which were staged in the patent theatres. Yet the nationalism that was creeping into Robin Hood portrayals was briefly subverted at the end of the eighteenth century, for the chapter entitled 'Revolution and Romanticism' examines the appearance of a revolutionary Robin Hood in the writings of late-eighteenth century English radicals. These texts had a transformative effect upon later portrayals of Robin Hood and imbued him with revolutionary ideology in which Robin Hood was said to have 'maintained a sort of independent sovereignty, and set kings, judges, and magistrates at defiance'. Thus, in 1795, the stage was set for future portrayals of the outlaw as a true warrior and friend of the people, and these ideas were adopted by the great Scottish writer Sir Walter Scott when he decided to write his own version of the Robin Hood story. Scott would then add new ideas into the legend, in particular that of Robin having been of Anglo-Saxon heritage. This is a trope which would reoccur in almost every retelling of the Robin Hood legend thereafter.

The Victorian period saw Robin Hood being reimagined many times, as we see in the sixth chapter. Many of the interpretations in this century were influenced by Scott's work. The most popular Victorian Robin Hood story, in Britain at least, was Pierce Egan the Younger's *Robin Hood and Little John; or, The Merry Men of Sherwood Forest* (1838–40). Written for an adult, working- and lower-middle-class audience, this weekly serial had it all: an exciting plot filled with sex, violence, and anti-establishment politics. It was so popular that it was reprinted many times throughout the Victorian period and into the twentieth century. It was also translated into French by the celebrated author, Alexandre Dumas, into two volumes as *Robin Hood the Outlaw* and *The Prince of Thieves* in the 1860s. Later on, the American illustrator, Howard Pyle, published *The Merry Adventures of Robin Hood* (1883), aimed at young readers. Pyle's book was also popular in Britain, but at the turn of the twentieth century, the main medium for the dissemination of new Robin Hood tales changed from texts to images, specifically moving images. While a few forgettable silent films were released in the 1910s in Britain and America (some of which are now lost), by the 1930s audiences could see and hear Robin Hood talking. Some filmmakers were quick to politicise the outlaw's story as had been done by novelists many times in the past. Thus we have perhaps the most famous visualisation of the Robin Hood story: Errol Flynn's *The Adventures of Robin Hood* (1938), which is subtly supportive of Franklin D. Roosevelt's New Deal, enacted between 1933 and 1937, which was a series of financial reforms designed to provide relief to the unemployed in Depression-era America and provide people with jobs, in order to get the economy moving again. Further Robin Hood movies and even television shows were released throughout the twentieth and twenty-first centuries, and these are discussed in the seventh and eighth chapters.

Thus, as the brief chapter overview makes clear, the Robin Hood story is one of continual renewal. Perhaps 'legend' is not the most appropriate term with which to describe a figure such as Robin Hood. In one sense, it might seem entirely appropriate given that the term, according to *The Oxford English Dictionary*, states that it is: 'A traditional story sometimes popularly regarded as historical but not authenticated'. Yet, as the brief synopsis given above indicates, there is not one story of Robin Hood but many stories that have circulated throughout history. Some stories say that Robin Hood was a nobleman, others say that he was a yeoman; some say he was noble and yet depict him as a brute; many stories say that he was an Anglo-Saxon freedom fighter while others make no mention of his ethnicity; Robin Hood has also been placed by various artists and writers in different time periods, ranging from the 1190s through to the fourteenth century.

The Legend of Robin Hood was therefore a convenient title for this book, but as will become clear throughout, it is often better to think of many of the stories told about Robin Hood throughout the centuries as being disconnected and entirely separate rather than a single corpus of poems, texts and films all telling the same story. While some writers certainly drew inspiration from previous portrayals of Robin Hood, it is often those authors who innovated and introduced entirely new narrative strands into the story who have had a significant and long-lasting influence on further depictions of Robin Hood. Let it be noted now, however, that when I speak of Robin Hood as being a figure who has, to a large extent, been shaped by popular culture, this should not always be taken to mean texts, plays, and films but also what scholars call 'material culture'. That term signifies physical objects and since the Victorian period Robin Hood has been represented in Staffordshire pottery and also, due to the popularity of twentieth-century movies, in action figures, such is the breadth of scope for continuing new and innovative ways in which authors, artists, writers, and even manufacturers have disseminated the story. With this in mind, let us now begin our journey through nearly 600 years of English social and cultural history and explore Robin Hood's portrayals in popular culture.

Note on Quotations

This book quotes numerous passages from late-medieval and early modern Robin Hood poems and ballads. All quotations are taken from the second edition Francis Child's *The English and Scottish Popular Ballads* (1882–98).

The translations I have given are intended for the benefit of the general reader and are not always literal, word-for-word translations, but are paraphrases intended to convey the meaning of a passage.

For transcriptions of the early texts, combined with full explanatory notes, I direct the reader to Stephen Knight and Thomas Ohlgren's *Robin Hood and Other Outlaw Tales* (1997), an open access resource which is available online via Rochester University's Robin Hood Project website.

Chapter 1

Medieval Poems

I can noughte parfitly my Paternoster as the prest it syngeth,
But I can rymes of Robyn Hood and Randalf Erle of Chestre.

William Langland, *Piers Plowman*, B Text (c. 1377)

While there are references to a man named Robin Hood in court records from as early as the 1220s, it is not until the fourteenth century that we find references to him in popular culture. As noted in the introduction, in the B-Text of William Langland's poem *Piers Plowman* (c. 1377), a lazy priest, who is the personification of the sin of Sloth, declares that he cannot recite the Lord's Prayer but he knows perfectly well rhymes of Robin Hood. The reference to 'rymes' indicates that by Langland's time, stories of Robin Hood were circulating among the populace (scholars have yet to definitively identify the second man named Randalf, although some historians have theorised that it refers to Ranulf, 3rd Earl of Chester). When Langland was writing, as Maurice Keen points out, these early rhymes were likely to have been simple, short refrains. These short stanzas would then have been added to by successive generations and they eventually developed into fully-fledged narratives. As to who originally composed them, nobody knows, for their authors' names are now lost in time. There may have been one composer, or the poems may have acquired various narrative strands from many different people until they reached the form that survives today. In England at this time, these stories were often spread by word of mouth, as it is likely that many of the people listening to stories of Robin Hood in the late-medieval period would have lacked the skills of reading and writing. Although this is not to say that medieval English society was completely illiterate; there were plenty of people who could read and write, but they mainly belonged to the upper classes. Thus, these early stories would have been recited and there is no evidence that medieval Robin Hood poems were set to music, as later seventeenth-century Robin Hood ballads would have been.

ROBIN HOOD

There are three extant early poems, all of which date in their present form from the mid-fifteenth century: *Robin Hood and the Monk*, *Robin Hood and the Potter*, and *A Gest of Robyn Hode*. They are some of the most interesting sources for any student of Robin Hood, and some of the narrative threads which appear in these early works reappear in depictions of the Robin Hood story in popular culture throughout subsequent centuries. Just in case anyone should get the wrong impression, however, it is necessary to acknowledge that each of these different poems did not depict the same Robin Hood. The outlaw who appeared in one poem was by no means meant to be the same as the one who appears in another. There is no evidence to suggest that the person who wrote down the *Gest*, for example, was also acquainted with *Robin Hood and the Potter*, and the Robin Hood of the *Gest* is much different to the one who appears in *Robin Hood and the Monk*. Let us take a look, then, at Robin Hood's first appearances in English popular culture.

As to who listened to these early poems, the first few lines of the *Gest* give some indication as to the social status of its audience:

Lythe and listin, gentilmen,	*Attend and listen, gentlemen,*
That be of frebore blode;	*That are of freeborn blood,*
I shall you tel of a gode yeman,	*I shall tell you of a good yeoman,*
His name was Robyn Hode.	*His name was Robin Hood.*

The poem does not address lowly serfs, or some vague idea of 'the commoner', but people that are 'of frebore blode'. The primary audience, of the *Gest* at least, were people based in urban areas, predominantly those in mercantile professions and trades. This is not to say definitively that the other two texts, *Robin Hood and the Monk*, and *Robin Hood and the Potter*, were enjoyed by the same types of people; neither of those two stories addresses 'gentilmen' in the same way that the opening of the *Gest* does, although they do not address the concerns of the poor either. It had been assumed by the mid-twentieth century Marxist historian, Rodney Hilton, that the early poems of Robin Hood were an expression of peasant discontent during the fourteenth century, the era of the so-called Peasants' Revolt of 1381. This seemed a bit far-fetched for James C. Holt, who hit back at Hilton's argument in the academic journal *Past and Present* and countered that there is nothing in the early texts of Robin Hood which suggests that he was at all interested in the problems of the peasants.

But Robin Hood allegedly stole from the rich and gave to the poor – so what of the poor? As Holt rightly argued, there is little in any of these early texts that indicates that Robin Hood is concerned with the problems of the people at large, and he certainly does not steal from the rich and redistribute their wealth to the destitute. The people whom Robin does help in the texts are not from the lower classes at all but of a higher rank: in the *Gest*, he lends money to a poor knight; in *Robin Hood and the Potter*, he compensates the potter, a tradesman, for money he has lost; in *Robin Hood and the Monk*, the outlaw does not help anyone financially at all but has to be rescued by Little John from the Sheriff. In these stories Robin is kind to the poor if he meets with them, but they are not his main concern. Instead of being tales for the poorer classes of people, therefore, these stories were actually entertainment for the gentry and yeomanry; these classes of people were higher than serfs but not a part of the nobility.

Thomas Ohlgren has researched in detail the social station of the people who recorded the texts for posterity which does, perhaps, give us an indication of who was listening to them. The owner of the manuscript containing the text of *Robin Hood and the Monk* was one Gilbert Pilkington, who was a clergyman from Lichfield. The manuscript of *Robin Hood and the Potter* was owned by a man named Richard Call, who was, like Robin Hood, a yeoman, though presumably not an outlaw. This does not preclude the possibility, of course, that commoners could have heard such tales in certain social settings; one manner in which the poorer classes could have encountered the stories of the ballads, if not the ballads themselves, was in Robin Hood village plays. Clearly no single audience can be attributed to the early 'rymes of Robyn Hode', and the fact that *Robin Hood and the Monk* was owned by a clergyman is surprising when the clergy as a whole receive a negative reputation in the *Monk*. Robin Hood, even at this early stage, was, it seems, 'all things to all men'. Everyone could enjoy his story, whether the listener was rich or poor, noble or serf.

The first thing which strikes any reader of these early texts is the fact that Robin Hood is not depicted as an earl, as he is commonly depicted in modern portrayals of the legend, but as a yeoman. For want of a better description, a yeoman was a member of the late-medieval middle classes comprising small-scale landholders and farmers, as well as the aforementioned urban tradesmen. There are very few descriptions of Robin's appearance in any of the ballads and they do not say what he looked like, other than that he dressed in green. Yeomen, even those who were not outlaws, often dressed in green clothing. This was particularly the case if they were foresters. These were people who maintained the royal forests and policed them, for they were given authority to arrest anyone whom they caught poaching. In his prologue to *The Canterbury Tales* (c. 1387), Geoffrey Chaucer gives us a more detailed description of a yeoman who is employed as a knight's servant:

A yeman hadde he and servantz namo
At that tyme, for hym liste ride soo;
And he was clad in cote and hood of grene.
A sheef of pecok arwes, bright and kene
Under his belt he bar ful thriftily,
(Wel koude he dresse his takel yemanly: Hise arwes drouped noght with fetheres lowe)
And in his hand he baar a myghty bowe.
A not heed hadde he, with a broun visage,
Of woodecraft wel koude he al the usage.
Upon his arm he baar a gay bracer,
And by his syde a swerd and a bokeler,
And on that oother syde a gay daggere
Harneised wel and sharpe as point of spere.
A Cristopher on his brest of silver sheene.
An horn he bar, the bawdryk was of grene;
A forster was he, soothly, as I gesse.

[The Knight] *only had a yeoman for a servant*
For it pleased him to travel thus,
And he wore a green coat and hood.
A sheaf of peacock arrows, bright and keen,
He carried under his belt,
(He took care of his equipment As all yeomen should because the feathers did not fall out of his arrows)
In his hand be beared a mighty bow
His hair was cropped, he had a browned face,
He was good at woodcraft
And wore a fine wrist guard on his arm,
By his side was a sword and a buckler,
And on the other side an elegant dagger,
With a point as sharp as a spear.
He wore a St Christopher on his breast,
He had a horn, his shoulder strap was green,
I guess he was a forester.

Robin Hood and the Monk is generally regarded as the oldest Robin Hood text in existence (it had no title when it was first written down, and the current title was assigned to it by nineteenth-century historians). Research conducted by Thomas Ohlgren indicates it has existed in manuscript form since c. 1465. And it is one of the scholars' favourite poems: the American scholar, Francis J. Child (1825–96), remarked of *Robin Hood and the Monk* that 'too much could not be said in praise of this ballad … it is very perfection in its kind'. The story begins on a bright Whitsuntide morning:

In somer, when þe shawes be sheyne,	*In the summer when the woods are bright,*
And leves be large and long,	*And the leaves are fully grown,*
Hit is full mery in feyre foreste,	*It is merry in the fair forest*
To here þe foulys song.	*To hear the birds sing.*

Robin decides that he must go and hear Mass because he has not done so in a while, so he decides to go to church in Nottingham. Much the Miller's son advises Robin that he should take some of his fellow yeomen with him for protection but Robin thinks taking only Little John will be sufficient. On the way to Nottingham, the pair decide to have an archery match and place wagers upon who will win. Surprisingly, John wins the match and five shillings from Robin, but Robin is not happy and loses his temper with John. John sulks off saying that he refuses to be his man anymore.

Robin finds himself having to attend Mass in Nottingham alone. During the service, a monk recognises Robin Hood and makes a discreet exit from the service to go and tell the Sheriff that the notorious outlaw is in Nottingham:

'Rise vp,' he said, 'þou prowde schereff,	*'Rise up,' he said, 'rise up you proud sheriff,*
Buske þe and make þe bowne;	*Quickly get ready;*
I haue spyed the kynggis felon,	*I have spotted the famous outlaw*
Ffor sothe he in þis town.	*Here in this town.*

'I haue spyed þe false felon,	*'I have seen the false felon,*
As he stondis at his masse;	*As he stood at Mass*
Hit is longe of þe,' seide þe munke,	*If you don't catch him,*
'And euer he fro vs passe.	*You'll only have yourself to blame.*

'þis traytur name is Robyn Hode,	*'This traitor's name is Robin Hood,*
Vnder þe greene-wode lynde,	*Once in the forest,*
He robbyt me onys a hundred	*He robbed me of a hundred*
pound,	*pounds,*
Hit shall neuer out of my mynde.'	*Which I shall never forget.'*

The Sheriff of Nottingham, eagerly wanting to catch this notorious Robin Hood, summons a number of armed men and leads them to the church. It is now that Robin misses Little John. Robin does manage to fight off many of the sheriff's men singlehandedly, but when he attacks the sheriff his sword breaks upon his head (we can assume here that the sheriff was perhaps wearing a helmet):

His sword vpon þe schireff hed,	*His sword upon the sheriff's head,*
Sertanly he brake in too:	*He broke in two.*
'þe smyth þat þe made,' seid	*'The smith that made you,' said*
Robyn,	*Robin,*
'I pray to God wyrke hym woo.'	*'I pray God brings you woe.'*

Robin is then arrested, and news of his capture reaches the outlaws who are at first despondent because their leader is gone and sure to face certain death for being an outlaw. Little John rouses them, however, and assures them that the Virgin Mary will never forsake their master. The outlaws learn that a monk has set off to carry news of Robin's capture to the king, so they decide to intercept the monk as he travels through the forest. The monk is travelling with a young page when the outlaws attack. They take the letters and in their treatment of the victims after the robbery the outlaws show their brutality:

John smote of þe munkis hed,	*John cut off the monk's head,*
No longer wolde he dwell;	*He would not live any longer.*
So did Much þe litull page,	*Much also killed the little page,*
Ffor ferd lest he wolde tell.	*For fear that he would tell.*

'Good' outlaws they may be, but there is little mercy for people like the monk and those who associate with corrupt clerics. The outlaws then travel to see the king to tell him that Robin Hood has been captured, but the king wants to punish Robin himself so he gives his seal to Little John with a commandment that Robin be brought before him unharmed, and the king pays the outlaws £20 for completing the task.

    Little John then arrives back in Nottingham, shows the seal to the sheriff, and conveys the king's instructions. The sheriff accepts the king's will and he and John share a few drinks, the sheriff gets quite drunk and needs to go to bed. While the sheriff is sleeping, John enters the jail, kills the porter, and sets Robin free. The pair of them then scale the walls of the castle and make their escape to the forest.

What is interesting about *Robin Hood and the Monk* is the fact that Robin is not necessarily the undisputed leader of the outlaws. Later portrayals, especially from the nineteenth century onwards, usually depict Robin Hood as the natural leader of the outlaws, often as a result of the fact that he is a nobleman. This is especially so in films such as *Robin Hood: Prince of Thieves* (1991). Yet there is a sense that one can rise in status in the early outlaw band through merit for after Little John has rescued Robin Hood, the latter seems prepared to resign his position as leader so that John can take over. Yet John does not want this, preferring merely to be a 'fellow' in the band and so Robin remains the leader.

The text of another early poem entitled *Robin Hood and the Potter* exists in a manuscript that can be dated to c. 1468. In this text, the outlaws come across as pretty inept at stopping people and actually robbing them, a theme which is incorporated into many modern portrayals of the Robin Hood story, when Robin meets somebody new he often has a playful fight with them first, in which he is beaten. This is known as a Robin-Hood-meets-his-match scenario. Robin Hood and Little John catch sight of a potter travelling with his wares on his way to Nottingham. At the time the poem was written down, pottery was a trade largely based in rural areas, and they would often travel to the town, like the potter does in the text, to sell their goods. The potter whom Robin and John encounter is the same potter who gave John a good hiding a little while back, and no outlaw has yet managed to extract any payment from the hardy potter. So John bets Robin forty shillings that he will not be able to best him in a fight. Robin Hood then stops the potter in his tracks:

There thes money they leyde,	*Thus they laid the money down,*
They toke het a yeman to kepe,	*They gave it to a yeoman to keep.*
Roben beffore the potter he breyde,	*Robin jumped in front of the potter,*
And bad hem stond still.	*And bade him stand still.*

Robin reminds the potter that he has not yet had the opportunity to pay pavage for the privilege of passing unmolested. Pavage was a tax levied by local town authorities in the Middle Ages for the specific purpose of road repairs. Local authorities could not raise these just as and when they pleased, however; they had to first apply to the king for permission to levy it. There were other taxes which could be raised in one off payments for specific purposes such as pontage, for the repair of bridges, and murage, for the repair of town walls. The system of raising taxes in this manner was widely disliked by the local populace and it was viewed as a means through which local officials could line their own pockets. In 1301, when Edward I was at Lincoln, he issued a licence to the town to collect pavage for the maintenance of the surrounding roads. Yet in 1313, we see auditors inspecting the town's accounts because the collectors had not carried out the works but had merely pocketed the money. It is no surprise, then, that when Robin asks the potter to pay pavage, he is bitterly reluctant to do so. The potter completely disregards Robin's demands and reaches for his staff and a short fight ensues. The potter then knocks Robin's buckler out of his hand and Robin admits that he has been beaten, no doubt to the amusement of Little John who is watching close by.

In a good-natured manner, Robin proposes that the potter becomes friends with the outlaws, to which the latter readily assents. Upon observing his cart, Robin asks the potter to exchange clothes with him and allow him to take his wares to Nottingham. While there, he sells all of the pottery, apart from five items, at a loss. The remaining ones he sends to the sheriff's house as a gift for the sheriff's wife. Very pleased with such a generous gift, the sheriff's wife invites Robin to dinner. After dinner with both the sheriff and his wife, an archery contest is held which Robin wins by splitting the arrow. The sheriff obviously has no idea that the potter sharing a meal with him is actually Robin Hood, and Robin tells the sheriff that he will help him catch the notorious outlaw by leading him into the woods. The sheriff gleefully assents and the next morning Robin and the Sheriff ride into the woods in order to catch Robin Hood. Once they arrive, Robin blows his horn and all the outlaws surround the sheriff. Had he known that the potter was Robin himself, the sheriff exclaims, he would never have consented to come to the forest. The outlaws make the sheriff leave all his possessions and his horse with them, so the sheriff has to travel back home on foot, although because Robin is fond of the sheriff's wife, he later sends her a gift of a horse. Robin then hands the potter £10 which more than compensates him for the loss of his wares.

By far the longest and most influential early Robin Hood text is *A Gest of Robyn Hode* (the word 'gest' means 'things done'). The poem was first printed by the London-based publisher, Richard Pynson, dated c. 1495. A further six editions, or copies that have survived to the present day at any rate, were then printed throughout the sixteenth century by a variety of publishers. The story is an amalgamation of several Robin Hood tales which, at some point before it was printed, were given unity by a now unknown compiler. The *Gest* begins in Barnsdale, with Robin leaned against a tree. The outlaws are hungry, as is Robin Hood himself, but Robin says that he will not dine until he has some unknown guest to share a meal with. Ideally, Robin would like a knight or a squire who can pay for the privilege of having a meal with Robin. Before the outlaws go in search of a guest for Robin, he lays down some general rules for the outlaws to observe while living in the greenwood:

Robyn loved Oure dere Lady:	*Robin loved our dear Lady,*
For dout of dydly synne,	*For doubt of deadly sin,*
Wolde he never do compani harme	*He would never harm any group,*
That any woman was in.	*In which women were found.*
'Maistar,' than sayde Lytil Johnn,	*'Master,' then said Little John,*
'And we our borde shal sprede,	*'If we are to spread our table,*
Tell us wheder that we shal go,	*Tell us where we shall go,*
And what life that we shall lede.	*And what life we shall lead.*
'Where we shall take, where we shall leve,	*'Where we shall take, where we shall leave,*
Where we shall abide behynde;	*Where we shall wait behind,*
Where we shall robbe, where we shal reve,	*Where we shall rob, were we shall despoil,*
Where we shall bete and bynde.'	*Where we shall beat and bind.'*
'Therof no force,' than sayde Robyn;	*'No matter,' then said Robin,*
'We shall do well inowe;	*'We will do well enough,*
But loke ye do no husbonde harme,	*But harm no husbandman,*
That tilleth with his ploughe.	*That tills the ground with a plough.*
'No more ye shall no gode yeman	*'Do not harm yeoman either,*
That walketh by grene wode shawe,	*That walks by the greenwood,*
Ne no knyght ne no squyer	*Neither knights nor squires,*
That wol be a gode felawe.	*That would be good fellows.*
'These bisshoppes and these archebishoppes,	*'But of these bishops and those archbishops,*
Ye shall them bete and bynde;	*You're permitted to beat and bind them*
The hye sherif of Notyingham,	*The High Sheriff of Nottingham,*
Hym holde ye in your mynde.'	*Hold him in your mind.'*

As Maurice Keen points out, to the poor and those of middling social status, the outlaws will show courtesy, but the representatives of corrupt institutions such as the church and local government shall receive no mercy. This is the first fully articulated statement of Robin's social mission, although there is nothing yet which indicates that Robin Hood makes a point of stealing from the rich to give to the poor.

The outlaws come across a poor knight, named Sir Richard of the Lee, travelling on his own through the forest. He looks as though he is in a sorry state, indicated by his scruffy, threadbare livery and also the fact that he does not have a servant travelling with him. Clothing in the medieval period was an important signifier of social rank, and these distinctions of dress and social status were demarcated in the sumptuary laws of the period. These laws also covered other items such as food, jewellery, and even the drinks of which person was allowed to partake. The possession of a fine livery and the ability to maintain a servant was a strong indicator of a knight's social status in the Middle Ages, and it is evident that this knight has lost all of these. Little John tells the knight that his master, Robin, has been waiting for him, and the knight assents to sharing a meal with the outlaws. After sharing a meal of bread, wine, and venison, Robin then asks the knight to pay for the meal. The knight reveals that he cannot pay because he is in debt to the Abbot of York to the tune of £400. This is because he has mortgaged his lands to the abbot to pay the bail for his son who had killed a knight at Lancaster. He has not a penny to his name and his trip to York is being made in the forlorn hope that the abbot will grant him more time to pay up. When it came to financial matters in the Middle ages, the church was often viewed as corrupt and avaricious. In Chaucer's *Friar's Tale*, the friar tells a story of a summoner who cons people out of money, and particular attention is drawn to the summoner's bribery of an old widow. There are also strong anti-clerical sentiments in Langland's *Piers Plowman*. While Jewish people had dominated the money-lending business in the time of Richard I and earlier, by the time the *Gest* was likely composed in the mid-fifteenth century, the church often lent money and acted as a debt collector as well, conveniently forgetting the Old Testament's prohibition of the sin of usury.

Little John searches the knight's belongings and it is evident that he is telling the truth. Impressed with his honesty, Robin decides to lend the knight £400 to repay his debt and makes the knight swear upon the Virgin Mary that he will repay the debt in one year's time. He also provides the knight with new clothes, and even tells him to take John to serve as his servant.

Little John and Sir Richard arrive at the Abbey of York to repay the £400. The knight pretends to still be bankrupt and ask for more time in order to test whether the abbot is a good man. The greedy abbot refuses so the knight exclaims,

'Haue here thi gold, sir abbot,' saide the knight,	*'Here take your gold, sir abbot,' said the knight,*
'Which that thou lentest me:	*'Which you let me borrow,*
Had thou ben curtes at my comynge,	*Had you been courteous to me,*
Rewarded shuldest thou haue be.'	*I would have rewarded you.'*

Little John and the knight then go their separate ways. The knight returns home temporarily and makes a gift of bows and arrows to give to Robin when he returns to pay his debt.

Meantime, Little John, having assumed the alias of Raynolde Greenlefe, secures a position in the service of the Sheriff of Nottingham by virtue of his excellent archery skills having been witnessed. He gets into numerous fights with members of the sheriff's household. After a particularly nasty fight with the sheriff's cook, the pair make friends and he convinces him to join the outlaw band. Little John lures the Sheriff of Nottingham into the forest upon the pretence of taking him hunting, but instead he leads him to Robin Hood. Robin toys with him, saying first that he must live out a year as an outlaw, and then tells him that he will spare the sheriff's life so long as he swears an oath to never harm any of Robin's men again.

A year to the day that Robin allowed Sir Richard to borrow £400, Robin awaits the return of the knight. He fears that the Virgin Mary is angry with him because the knight has not shown. As it happens, the High Cellarer of the Abbot of St Mary's, York, is travelling through the forest that day bearing £800. Robin and his men take the money from him; Robin is pleased because the fact that this monk has come from St Mary's carrying more than enough money to repay the knight's debt means that the Virgin Mary is pleased with Robin. The monk is then sent on his way, considerably lighter in purse. After a short while Sir Richard also returns and apologises to Robin for his lateness. But it is now of no consequence, the knight's debt does not need to be repaid because the Virgin Mary has already repaid it. In fact, in his generosity, Robin gives the knight a further £400 in order to equip himself properly with a new horse.

Shortly afterwards, the sheriff holds an archery contest. Robin is determined to participate in it so he does so in disguise. The prize is a gold and silver arrow, and of course Robin wins the contest by splitting another contestant's arrow. Just after he collects the arrow, somebody recognises him and summons the men-at-arms to pursue Robin and the other outlaws in attendance. A fight ensues in which the outlaws manage to kill a number of the sheriff's men, but Little John is wounded. Instead of going back to the greenwood they decide to go to the castle of Sir Richard, who readily receives them in return for services offered. The sheriff and his men must have been hot on the outlaws' heels, however, because he surrounds Sir Richard's castle. An ineffective siege ensues and, realising that he cannot win, the sheriff travels to see the king in London to ask his advice on what to do with Sir Richard.

After the siege has ended, Robin and the outlaws return to the greenwood. The sheriff with instructions from the king comes to arrest Sir Richard, who is bound by hands and feet and taken to Nottingham. Sir Richard's wife at once notifies the outlaw of what has happened, and Robin resolves to rescue him. Robin kills the sheriff by cutting off his head and takes Sir Richard back to the greenwood. King Edward then travels to Nottingham to go hunting in the royal forest. The king becomes enraged, not because Robin has killed his sheriff, but because there are hardly any deer to hunt. He resolves once and for all to capture Robin, and the following episode relates a fairly typical 'king and commoner' encounter, which is why we cannot assume the *Gest* relates to any actual historical events. The king and his men dress as monks and venture into the forest where they meet with Robin and the outlaws. The conversation takes various turns, with Robin confessing that out of every man in England he loves King Edward the most. They share a feast on the king's deer, no doubt to the king's grudging approval, and then an archery contest is held which the king wins. After the contest, King Edward reveals his identity to the outlaws who immediately bow in front of him. The king, impressed with Robin's loyalty, invites him to serve at court, a request to which Robin readily assents.

The king's treatment of Robin Hood has parallels with another outlaw tale entitled *Adam Bell, Clym of the Clough, and William of Cloudesley* (1557–58). At the end of their ballad, the king, who is not identified (as in the *Gest*) invites them to serve him at court. A cynical reading of these plots suggests that the king in the *Gest* wants to contain and neuter Robin Hood. In medieval and early modern societies, in which law enforcement was weak, it was not unusual for the state to co-opt former criminals into their employment. This often happened in late-medieval Eastern Europe, as

Kelly Hignett's research has shown, where bandits were employed as border guards. In the *Gest*, the king had clearly grown tired of allowing Robin and his men to terrorise the forest and hunt all of the deer, so he has adopted a policy of keeping his friends close and his enemies even closer.

Robin stays at court for twelve months, but he soon grows tired of the lifestyle. Besides, he can barely afford to keep up with the extravagant lifestyle as a member of the court. While the king's pardoning of Robin does mirror many of the rewards given out in king and commoner tales, Truesdale points out that often in such tales the reward turns out to be onerous for the commoner. This is the same in the *Gest*. Having grown tired of life at the court, Robin asks the king if he can return briefly to Barnsdale forest; Robin had built a chapel to Mary Magdalene in the forest and longs to worship there. The king allows him to return for a short while but, once back in Barnsdale, nostalgia for his old way of life overtakes him; he blows on his horn and immediately seven score yeomen outlaws appear, glad that their master has returned. In what must surely be the first literary portrayal of what criminologists today would call 'recidivism' (reoffending), Robin never returns to the king's service but instead remains an outlaw.

However, Robin was not portrayed as totally invincible in the *Gest*. He stays in Barnsdale for another twenty years when, feeling ill, he goes to be bled by the Prioress of Kirklees. She is in league with one of Robin's enemies named Sir Roger of Doncaster, and they conspire to kill Robin, although the *Gest* does not reveal too many details about how they do this. A later early modern ballad, entitled *Robin Hood's Death*, reveals the manner of the betrayal, which was that the prioress let out too much blood. Richard Grafton's *Chronicle at Large*, from 1569, likewise reveals that this was the manner of Robin Hood's death:

> But in an olde an auncient Pamphlet I finde this written of the sayd Robert Hood … For the sayd Robert Hood, beyng afterwardes troubled with sicknesse, came to a certein Nonry in Yorkshire called Bircklies, where desiryng to be let blood, he was betrayed & bled to death. After whose death the Prioresse of the same place caused him to be buried by the high way side, wher he had vsed to rob and spoyle those that passed that way. And vpon his graue the sayde Prioresse did lay a very fayre stone, wherein the names of Robert Hood, William of Goldesborough, and others were grauen.

As we have seen, the 'olde and auncient Pamphlet' to which Grafton referred was probably the *Gest* itself. In the *Gest*, Robin subsequently dies and the poem ends with the following benediction:

Cryst have mercy on his soule,	*Christ have mercy on his soul,*
That dyed on the rode,	*That died on the cross,*
For he was a good outlawe,	*For he was a good outlaw,*
And dyde pore men moch god.	*And did poor men much good.*

The dates given above are the years from which the physical manuscripts or early printed editions of the poems existed. This does not preclude the stories discussed here having existed in some form before they were written down, although any attempt to date the poems through linguistics is really just a matter of speculation. Throughout the twentieth century, scholars were content to stay safe with giving generalised dates of origin for many of the early Robin Hood texts, most often preferring to stay in the region of c. 1450, although some, such as Maurice Keen, did assign a date as early as c. 1400 for the composition of some of the *Gest*.

In one respect, in fact, these late-medieval stories of Robin Hood were already 'historical' when they were first recorded. The sentence of outlawry had lost much of its potency by the late fourteenth and fifteenth centuries. It was a sentence that existed prior to the establishment of the legal precepts of habeas corpus. It fell into disuse by the late medieval period because the social and legal system of England was changing from one that was based upon the exclusion and summary punishment of felons, to one which increasingly favoured custodial sentences. Thus, certainly by the time that the *Gest* was printed, it would have been rare to find somebody who had been placed beyond the law: in the early modern period all people were subject to the law.

Robin Hood and the Monk, *Robin Hood and the Potter*, and *A Gest of Robyn Hode*, of course, are clearly identifiable texts about the outlaw from the Middle Ages. However, there are some other extant texts which depict the story of an outlaw in the forest named Robin, but around which some debate exists concerning their canonicity. Other texts, such as the manuscript for a tale entitled *Robin Hood and Guy of Gisborne* do not physically date from the period, but similar stories were in circulation during the late medieval period. We know this because, luckily, some of the scripts for Robin Hood village plays telling those stories have survived.

Chapter 2

Medieval Plays and Ballads

Robyn bent his joly bowe,
Þer in he set a flo;
Þe fattest der of alle
Þe herte he clef a to.

Robin and Gandeleyn (c. 1450)

Robin Hood and the Monk, Robin Hood and the Potter, and *A Gest of Robyn Hode* are what we can identify as bona fide medieval poems. Debates exist as to the exact dating of the composition of those texts, but they were all recorded in writing towards the end of the fifteenth century. However, there is another set of texts which some Robin Hood scholars are reluctant to include within the canon of early texts.

The story of Robin Hood's death at the hands of the scheming Prioress of Kirklees was known by the time that the *Gest* was printed. The story was then repeated in the early modern ballad entitled *The Death of Robin Hood*. A different story of the death of a forest dwelling man named Robin Hood appeared before the *Gest*. While *Robin Hood and the Monk* is generally considered to be the oldest Robin Hood text in existence, from around 1450 there appeared a poem called *Robyn and Gandeleyn*. The similarities between this and contemporary Robin Hood ballads are noteworthy: as its title implies, it features a Robin, along with a man named Gandeleyn, who are in the forest hunting for deer. Gandeleyn is a corrupted version of Gamelyn, who appears in a Middle English Romance entitled *The Tale of Gamelyn*, dated c. 1350. In this tale, Gamelyn is forced to become an outlaw after he kills his overbearing brother at a meal; he takes to the forest where he comes face to face with an unnamed 'master outlaw', although there is no indication that the master outlaw here is meant to be Robin Hood.

In *Robyn and Gandelyn*, Robin is rather unceremoniously shot and killed with an arrow:

There cam a schrewde arwe out of the west,	*There came an arrow straight out of the west,*
That felde Robertes pryde.	*That struck Robert down dead.*

Gandeleyn looks around and sees the shooter, named Wrennock, whom Gandeleyn subsequently kills for having murdered Robin. The Robin who appears in *Robyn and Gandeleyn* is admittedly never named as Robin Hood in the actual poem, which is rather short and resembles a ballad or a song, rather than a long narrative poem such as the *Gest*. The surviving manuscript, in fact, is contained within a collection of carols and lyric poems. While there are no compelling reasons to doubt that *Robyn and Gandeleyn* is a Robin Hood tale—for who else but *the* Robin Hood would be in the forest shooting at deer—debate among scholars as to its canonicity exists to this day.

Robin Hood and Guy of Gisborne is one of the most interesting Robin Hood tales to have survived. The earliest surviving version of this can be dated to the seventeenth century and was first printed for wide readership in Thomas Percy's *Reliques of Ancient English Poetry* (1765). *Robin Hood and Guy of Gisborne* might have been lost to history completely had Percy not rescued the manuscript, among others, from being burned by a housemaid who wanted to use the paper to light the fire. Percy remarked that the poem 'carries marks of much greater antiquity than any of the popular songs on [Robin Hood]'. The other popular songs which Percy referred to in that passage were the printed broadsides of Robin Hood ballads that date from the seventeenth century. A. J. Pollard similarly argues that, although the extant text dates from the early modern period, by its content and language it can be dated to the mid-fifteenth century. The story of Robin Hood's encounter with Guy of Gisborne begins in the following manner:

When shawes beene sheene, and shradds full fayre,	*When the forest is bright, and the branches are full,*
And leaves both large and longe,	*And the leaves are large and long.*
Itt is merrye walking in the fayre forrest,	*It is indeed merry walking in the fair forest*
To hear the small birds songe.	*To hear the small birds sing.*

The woodweele sang and wold not cease,	*The woodweele sang without ceasing.*
Amongst the leaues a lyne,	*Amongst the leaves of the lime tree.*
And it is by two wight yeomen	*And it is by two strong yeomen,*
By deare God, that I mean.	*By dear God that I mean.*

The leaves are bright and green, the birds are singing. It is a fairly pleasant scene. Had the ballad truly only dated from the seventeenth century, it is unlikely that the celebration of the forest, found in both *Robin Hood and the Potter* and *Robin Hood and the Monk*, would have been copied in *Robin Hood and Guy of Gisborne*. Later ballads very rarely commence with a celebration of forest life. Yet in spite of the pleasing picture created, there is a sense of foreboding; an idea that the greenwood can switch from being a place of refuge to one of danger. Robin has had an uneasy night's sleep in which he dreamt, or rather had a premonition, of two sturdy yeoman, and it is the bird's chirping that has woken him. Little John tells him not to worry, for dreams come and go. Visibly shaken, however, along with Little John he decides to go searching for the yeoman who appeared in his dream. Eventually the pair come across a yeoman in the forest:

The cast on their gowne of greene,	*They put on their green clothes,*
A shooting gone are they,	*They are gone shooting.*
Vntill they came to the merry greenwood,	*Then they came to the merry greenwood,*
Where they had gladdest bee;	*Where they were glad to be.*
There were the ware of wight yeoman,	*There they saw a strong yeoman,*
His body leaned to a tree.	*He was leaning against a tree.*
A sword and a dagger he wore by his side,	*He wore both a sword and a dagger,*
Had beene many a mans bane,	*Which had been the bane of many a man,*
And he was cladd in a capull-hyde,	*And he was wearing a capull-hyde*
Topp, and tayle, and mayne	*From head to toe.*

In a similar manner to occurrences in *Robin Hood and the Monk*, Little John and Robin Hood have a dispute and part ways. The argument is over a relatively minor matter: John wants to be the first to approach the man and Robin commands him not to, saying,

ROBIN HOOD

A, Iohn, by me thou setts noe store,	*John, you must not think much of me,*
And that's a ffarley thinge;	*And that's surprising.*
How offt send I my men before,	*How often do I send my men ahead*
And tarry myself behind?	*And wait myself behind?*

[...]	[...]

But often words they breeden bale,	*Because words often cause grief,*
That parted Robin and Iohn;	*Robin and John parted ways.*
Iohn is gone to Barnesdale,	*John then went to Barnsdale,*
The gates he knowes eche one.	*He knows the way there.*

Alone, Robin approaches the man but does not reveal his identity. The man, Guy of Gisborne, is a bounty hunter who has been hired for the sum of £40 by the Sheriff of Nottingham to hunt down and kill Robin Hood. Robin then offers to be Guy's guide through the forest and promises to lead him to Robin Hood. Although there are debates about the exact dating of this poem, in the medieval period some men did often offer to track down outlaws and thieves for local officials in reward for cash. A man named Roger de Wensley was hired to track down the notorious Folville gang who had been terrorising the inhabitants of Rutland and Leicestershire, although in this case it did not work out very well for the authorities as Wensley just ended up joining the gang.

Meantime, back in Barnsdale, John has returned to find one of the outlaws, William a Trent, slain by the sheriff's men. The sheriff is also present and binds John to a tree, and promises him that he will soon hear news that Robin Hood has been killed. And a much worse punishment is in store for John. The sheriff menacingly promises him that,

'Thou shalt be drawen by dale and downe,' quoth the sheriff,	*'You will be drawn by dale and down,' said the Sheriff,*
'And hanged hye on a hill.'	*And hanged high on the hill.'*
'But thou may ffayle,' quoth Little Iohn,	*'O may you fail,' said Little John,*
'If itt be Christs owne will.'	*'If it be Christ's will.'*

The poem then switches back to Robin and Guy, with Robin challenging Guy to a shooting match, which Robin naturally wins. Guy commends Robin on his excellent marksmanship and then asks his name. Robin reveals his identity and immediately the two men draw swords and begin fighting:

He that had neither kithe nor kin	*No one who had either kith or kin,*
Might haue seen a full fayre sight,	*Had seen such a fight as when*
To see how together these yeomen went,	*These two yeoman started fighting,*
With blades both browne and bright.	*With swords drawn.*

Guy almost gets the better of Robin when he stumbles on a branch and falls to the floor. It looks like all might be over for him until the Virgin Mary gives him the courage to fight on:

Robin thought on Our Lady deere,	*Robin thought upon Our Lady dear*
And soon leapt vp againe,	*And soon leapt up again,*
And thus he came with an awkward stroke,	*And thus he came with an awkward stroke*
Good Sir Guy hee has slayne.	*Good Sir Guy he had slain.*

Robin then takes his knife and decapitates Sir Guy and mutilates his face so it is almost unrecognisable. He then places Guy's head on the end of his bow and dons Guy's clothes. He then blows on Guy's bugle horn in order to alert the sheriff that Robin has supposedly been killed (these early poems often contain plot-holes, and it is not known how or why Robin would have known that the Sheriff was keeping Little John hostage). Robin then arrives back at the camp where Little John and the Sheriff are waiting and Robin, in disguise as Guy, tells the Sheriff,

'But now I haue slaine the master,' he sayd,	*'And I have slain the master,' he said,*
'Let me goe strike the knaue;	*'Let me strike his knave;*
This is all the reward I aske,	*This is the only reward I ask*
Nor noe other will I haue.'	*I don't want anything else.*

'Thou art a madman,' said the shiriffe,	*'You're a madman,' said the sheriff,*
'Thou shouldest haue a knights ffee,	*You should a knight's fee,*
Seeing thy asking hath beene so badd,	*But as you're desperately asking,*
Well granted it shall be.'	*I grant you your request.'*

To the sheriff's surprise, Robin cuts the rope in which John is bound. The sheriff then attempts to flee but as he is making his escape, Robin hands Guy's bow to John and fires an arrow into the sheriff's back which 'did cleaue his heart in twain'.

While it is argued that the text of *Robin Hood and Guy of Gisborne* dates from the seventeenth century, a similar story was definitely known during the late-medieval period. A fragment of a play entitled *Robyn Hod and the Shryff of Notygnham* survives and can be dated to c. 1475. The date of origin can be stated with a degree of accuracy because the manuscript upon which the play survives contains the accounts of a man named John Sterndalle for the period 1475–76. The same play is also referenced in a letter from John Paston in 1473, who complains that his servant, who was to play Robin Hood in one such game, has left him without a replacement. Two other early plays survive to the present day because William Copland's edition of the *Gest*, published in 1550, contains an appendix entitled *The Playe of Robyn Hode verye proper to be played in Maye Games*. The Copland edition that has survived is incomplete. However, it does contain an almost complete version of the text of a play titled *Robin Hood and the Friar*, as well as a fragment of another play obviously based upon the story of *Robin Hood and the Potter*. The plays would have been performed at village fairs, dances, ales, and pageants, usually held in spring or through the summer. In pre-industrial England, the warmer seasons were a joyful time people could come together and celebrate the passing of a harsh winter. Money was often raised at these events in aid of local issues, such as fixing church roofs and other ad hoc maintenance jobs, so the idea that Robin Hood stole from the rich and gave to the poor could have gradually emerged from these charitable occasions.

Plays could have both secular and religious themes, and in the former category Robin Hood plays featured prominently. In fact, at certain times of the year, seeing a Robin Hood play was deemed to be more important to villagers than hearing the word of God. In 1549, Bishop Hugh Latimer related how he once visited a village to preach a sermon only to find the church doors locked. A villager informed him that,

> 'Sir, this is a busy day with us, we cannot hear you; it is Robin Hood's day. The parish are gone abroad to gather for Robin Hood; I pray you let them not.' I was fain there to give place to Robin Hood ... It is no laughing matter, my friends, it is a weeping matter, a heavy matter; a heavy matter, under the pretence of gathering for Robin Hood, a traitor and a thief, to put out a preacher, to have his office less esteemed; to prefer Robin Hood before the ministration of God's word; and all this

hath come of unpreaching prelates. This realm hath been ill-provided for, that it hath such corrupt judgments in it, to prefer Robin Hood to God's word.

Clearly there was a time for worship, but Robin Hood had a day set aside as well. It has been theorised that plays of Robin Hood were actually more popular than ballads and, although very few fragments of the plays themselves survive, there are many records of plays of Robin Hood being staged. These plays were not only held in Yorkshire but as far afield as Exeter, which is where the earliest record of a play can be found, in 1426. The script of *Robyn Hod and the Shryff of Notyngham* contains no stage directions and is likely to have served as an approximate guide as to what performers should say, while allowing for a significant degree of improvisation by the actors; the occasions on which these types of plays were performed, after all, were social, enjoyable occasions, and it is entirely conceivable that when local villagers were playing the parts in front of their friends and neighbours there would have been some improvisation.

The free-flowing and largely improvised manner in which these plays were performed allowed other characters to enter the legend, notably Friar Tuck and Maid Marian. Both of these characters are *entirely* fictional, in spite of Mark Olly's recent work which claims to have identified a historical figure called Marian. So far, our discussion of medieval Robin Hood poems have not mentioned Maid Marian. There was a French pastoral play written by Adam le Hall entitled *Jeu de Robin et Marion* (c. 1283), which told the story of two lovers named Robin and Marian, but it is uncertain whether the Robin and Marian of this play were one and the same with Robin Hood and Maid Marian. *Robin et Marion* was a genteel pastoral but the village plays were not. But the elites certainly feared that the unruliness of the village plays could lead to unrest. In 1376, the poet John Gower, whose *Mirour de l'homme* was eerily prophetic of the Peasants' Revolt, condemned the often unruly village games over which the characters of Robin and Marion presided. The villager playing Marion was usually crowned the Queen of May in the May games. It would then fall to the sixteenth-century playwright, Anthony Munday, and the nineteenth-century novelist, Thomas Love Peacock, to cement Maid Marian's place in the Robin Hood legend.

In *Robyn Hod and the Shryff of Notyngham*, a knight approaches the sheriff and offers to kill Robin for a fee. Robin then enters and he and the knight begin a shooting match, which Robin wins. The pair of them fight without weapons, and then a sword fight ensues, which Robin wins by killing the knight. Robin then beheads him and puts his clothes on:

Now I haue the maystery here,	*I have mastery over him now,*
Off I smyte this sory swyre.	*I'll smite him at his neck.*
This knyghtys clothis wolle I were,	*I will wear this knight's clothes,*
And in my hode his hede woll bere.	*And I'll carry his head in my hood.*

The next part of the play is probably missing because the scene switches to Robin being held in gaol, along with two other outlaws, one of them named Friar Tuck. Everyone's favourite fighting monk appears to have had his own legend before being incorporated, in a rather convoluted way, into the Robin Hood story. In early Robin Hood stories, Friar Tuck was not the fat, jolly monk depicted today but a hardy, stout man of action. The name Friar Tuck first appeared, so contemporary accounts tell us, in Sussex. It was a soubriquet given to a criminal gang-leader named Robert Stafford in 1417, and the same Friar Tuck had managed to evade authorities until at least 1429, when his name appears again in court records. Tuck is certainly a man of fighting spirit in *Robyn Hod and the Shryff off Notyngham*. He singlehandedly fights the sheriff and helps the outlaws escape. After the outlaws escape, the play then ends abruptly.

Fryer Tucke appears in another medieval play entitled *Robin Hood and the Friar*, which is also appended to Copland's printed edition of the *Gest*. Here we see another side to the jolly friar – a very rude one at that! The tale is similar to the one told in an early modern ballad entitled *Robin Hood and the Curtal Friar*. Some debate exists as to the exact dating of the ballad, with the earliest complete edition surviving in an edition of *Robin Hood's Garland*, published in 1663 (printed 'garlands' were collections of songs arranged around a theme).

In both the ballad and the play Robin makes a strange request: he commands Tuck to carry him on his back across the river. After carrying Robin a very short distance, Tuck simply throws Robin into the water. He gets very annoyed with Tuck for this insolent act and a fight with quarterstaffs ensues; Tuck gets the better of Robin Hood, until, as we read in the ballad,

A boon, a boon, thou curtal frier,
I beg it on my knee;

Give me leave to set my horn to my mouth,
And to blow blasts three.

After a blast of his horn Robin's men then appear, but Tuck responds by summoning his pack of ravenous hounds. Robin diffuses the situation by asking Tuck to join his band of merry men, and the ballad ends by saying that,

This curtal frier had kept Fountains Dale
Seven long years or more;
There was neither knight, lord, nor earl
Could make him yield before.

The play takes us a little further: not only is Tuck promised money for joining the outlaws but he is also promised the company of a woman, which pleases him greatly:

Here is an huckle duckle	*My huckle duckle stretches*
An inche aboue the buckle	*An inch above my buckle,*
She is a trul of trust	*She is a trustworthy trollop*
to serue a friar at his lust	*To serve a horny friar,*
A prycker and a prauncer	*A pricker and a prancer,*
A terer of shetes	*A tearer of sheets,*
A wagger of ballockes	*A wagger of testicles*
When other men slepes	*When other men sleep.*
Go home ye knaues	*Go home you knaves*
And lay crabbes in the fyre	*And prepare the meal*
For my lady and I wil daunce	*For my lady and I will dance.*

While some may think of the 'ladye' that Tuck is offered is the character of Maid Marian, the actual text of the play does not mention her by name at all. Marian was certainly, as we have seen, a common figure featured in village May games, but there were many other characters as well.

The play of *Robin Hood and the Potter* likewise follows, approximately, the story found in the poem. Robin begins by addressing the audience:

Lysten to me, my merry men all,
And harke what I shall say,
Of an adventure I shall you tell,
That befell this other daye.

ROBIN HOOD

With a proude potter I met,
And a rose-garland on his head,
The floures of it shone marvellous freshe;
This seuen yere and more he hath used this waye,
Yet he was never so curteyse a potter,
As one penny passage to paye.
Is there any of my merry men all,
That dare be so bolde
To make this potter paie passage,
Either silver or golde?

The next person to speak in the play is Little John, played in all likelihood by a member of the village, who says that none of the outlaws have yet dared to stop the hardy potter. The potter comes along and refuses to pay, and threatens Robin saying 'take thy sword and thy buckeler in thy hande, / and se what shall befall'. A fight commences between Robin and the potter, with Little John also wanting to enter the fray. However, the play abruptly ends after John has sworn to put him to flight by saying, 'Be the knave never so stoute, I shall rappe him on the snoute, and put hym to flight'.

Village games of Robin Hood largely disappeared during the early modern period when Robin entered the world of Elizabethan high theatre. For people in more humble stations of life, Robin acquired a post-medieval 'afterlife' in the vulgar ballads which circulated during the seventeenth century. Let us take a look at an interesting period of transformations when Robin is raised from the humble status of a yeoman to that of a dispossessed aristocrat, becoming Robert, Earl of Huntingdon.

Chapter 3

The Early Modern Period

All in a woodman's jacket he was clad,
Of Lincolne Greene, belay'd with silver lace;
And on his head an hood with aglets sprad,
And by his side his hunters horne he hanging had.

Edmund Spenser, *The Faerie Queene* (1590–96)

This youth that leads yon virgin by the hand
Is our Earl Robert, or your Robin Hood
That in these days was Earl of Huntingdon;
The ill-fac'd miser, brib'd in either hand,
Is Warman, once the steward of his house,
Who, Judas like, betrays his liberal lord.

Anthony Munday, *The Downfall of Robert,
Earle of Huntington* (1597–98)

While village-based Robin Hood plays and games flourished in the late medieval and early modern period, they had become a thing of the past by the Jacobean era, as illustrated in the following ditty by a contemporary poet, who looks back nostalgically on times gone by:

Let us talk of Robin Hood,
And Little John in Merry Sherwood,
Of poet Skelton with his pen,
And many other merry men,
Of May-game Lords and Summer Queens
And milkmaids dancing o'er the greens.

Due to the fact that the texts of very few plays were written down, none of them had a sustained influence on successive portrayals of the Robin

25

Hood story. Robin did, very briefly however, appear in the world of high theatre in the early modern period, which is the name generally given to the sixteenth, seventeenth, and eighteenth centuries. The legend of Robin Hood underwent some interesting transformations during this time, in fact many medieval figures receive reputations that remain with them thereafter. William Shakespeare's *Richard III* (c. 1593), for example, portrayed the eponymous king as a deformed tyrant, an image of him which would reappear in successive representations of him and even, in the Victorian period, inform historical scholarship. It is during this time we first see Robin's status as an outlawed nobleman cemented in popular culture, which was first ascribed to him in Anthony Munday's two plays, *The Downfall of Robert, Earl of Huntington* and *The Death of Robert, Earl of Huntingdon* (1597–98), which were written with the possible assistance of Henry Chettle.

The Downfall is a play within a play. At the beginning we are introduced to John Skelton (c. 1463–1529) in his study. The real Skelton was the personal tutor of the young King Henry VIII and was later appointed Poet Laureate. In the play, he and Sir John Eltham are preparing for a rehearsal of *The Downfall*, and they need to get this right, for they must perform it in front of the king later. In a hurry, Skelton summons all the players, and the rehearsal begins.

The plot is essentially a love triangle between Robin Hood, Matilda (to be called Maid Marian later in the play), Queen Eleanor of Aquitaine, and Prince John. Robin Hood and Marian are devoted to each other, but the queen loves Robin and John loves Marian. Prince John is also plotting to assume the throne while his brother, Richard, is away fighting the crusades. Yet Earl Robin is loyal to Richard and will have no part of John's plan. The latter then conspires to have Robin arrested for debt and declared an outlaw. To do this, John conspires with Robin's steward, Warman, who is tasked with allowing the soldiers into Robin's house on his wedding night:

> *Enter Robin Hoode, little Iohn following him; the one earle of Huntington, the other his seruant, Robin hauing his napkin on his shoulder, as if he were sodainely raised from dinner.*
>
> > *Robin.* As I am outlawed from my fame and state,
> > By this day outlawed from the name of daies,
> > Day lucklesse, outlawe, lawlesse, both accurst.
>
> *Flings away his napkin, hat, and sitteth downe.*

Iohn. Doe not forget your honourable state,
Nor the true noblesse of your worthy house.

Robin is forced to forget his 'true noblesse' when he flees to the forest along with his bride, Matilda. After this, the pair assume the identities of Robin Hood and Maid Marian, and Robin casts aside any pretentions to nobility:

> *Rob*. Nay no more honour, I pray thee little Iohn,
> Henceforth I will be called Robin Hoode,
> Matilda shall be my Maid Marian.

They are eventually joined in the forest by the usual suspects, including Scarlet, Scathelock, and Much the Miller's Son. Friar Tuck is played by Skelton so he often breaks character and talks directly to the audience. Eventually John decides to stop trying to usurp Richard's throne because he heard a story about him killing a lion in Austria and concludes, perhaps wisely, that if Richard really is so brave then it is not a good idea to provoke him. This is a wise step by John because Richard soon returns and, as almost every Hollywood Robin Hood film depicts, pardons Robin Hood and restores his land to him.

The second play entitled *The Death of Robert, Earl of Huntingdon* takes place after Robin's restitution into royal favour, and it is a little ridiculous in parts. While Robin Hood, King Richard, Prince John, and the rest of the former outlaws are out hunting, Robin's uncle, the Prior of York, decides that he wants his nephew dead. He conspires with Sir Roger of Doncaster to kill him. The prior subsequently gives Robin a drink that contains poison after which, having given a speech that is 200 lines long saying goodbye to his friends and forgiving his former enemies, he finally dies. Richard I then dies almost immediately after Robin Hood and John is proclaimed as king. Just after Marian's husband has died is the perfect time, John thinks, to try and woo her again. Marian resists John's advances and escapes from him and takes refuge in Dunmow Abbey. Later on, John's misrule has caused a number of nobles to raise up arms against him, a subplot which is Munday's attempt to historicise the story of Robin Hood within the context of the Barons' rebellion against the historical King John which culminated in the passage of Magna Carta. John's love for Marian turns to anger, however, and so he sends an assassin after her named Brand. When Brand meets with Marian, he politely informs her that he has come to poison her. Instead of shrinking back in fear, Marian decides that, since the death of her beloved

Robin Hood, she too wishes to die and so willingly takes the poison. The assassin then feels so guilty about this deed that he hangs himself from the nearest tree. When King John learns of what has happened he is distraught and repents of all his former crimes and misdeeds, and the nobles, at seeing their king so upset, decide not to rebel against him anymore but swear loyalty to him.

Two plays which were written around the same time as Munday's entitled *Robin Hood and Little John* (1594) and *Robin Hood's Penn'orths* (1600) are now lost, so we do not know whether these plays likewise portrayed the outlaw as the Earl of Huntingdon. Another play from this period, a comedy entitled *Look About You* (1600) likewise depicts Robin Hood as being of noble heritage. *The Death of Robert* also appears to have been the inspiration for a play entitled *King John and Matilda* (1650). The question remains as to why Munday recast Robin as the Earl of Huntingdon. One possible explanation is that Munday probably mixed up his Barnsdales: there is a Barnsdale in Rutland and during the 1190s, which is when Munday set his play, the local lord, a man named David, who was the brother of the King of Scotland, was also the Earl of Huntingdon. Yet apart from this quite tenuous connection, which we do not know for certain that Munday even knew himself — as Rutland has very little association with the Robin Hood legend — Munday's mistake does not immediately invalidate assigning Barnsdale, Yorkshire as the area in which the *Gest* was set, and neither does it mean that there was no historical outlaw from Yorkshire.

Robin Hood scholars have previously emphasised the fact that Robin Hood was already acquiring the vague attributes of an idea of 'nobility' of character in late medieval chronicles. Formally making the outlaw an earl seemed to be the natural extension of his having been 'the most humane and the prince of all robbers'. Although it should be noted that in Munday's play, Robin does revert to being a yeoman once he is outlawed, as revealed in the passage which reads, 'nowe is Robert Hood, a simple yeoman as his servants were'. At the same time, however, Robin Hood had become so culturally powerful a figure, and 'all things to all men,' so to speak, that we even find accounts of Henry VIII dressing up as Robin Hood. In 1510, the young Henry apparently burst into the chambers of his wife, Catherine of Aragon, dressed in green suits and requested a dance. On May Day in 1515, Henry and his male courtiers once again dressed up as Robin Hood's merry men and rode, with Catherine, to Shooters Hill where they dined on venison and ale. Several of the courtiers in attendance played the parts of Maid Marian, Lady May, Friar Tuck, and Little John.

Yet to explain why Robin Hood was recast as an earl, a measure which had little precedent in earlier stories, the wider social and political context must be examined. The plays were written between 1597 and 1598. Often, in modern portrayals of the Elizabethan era, the period is portrayed as some type of 'Golden Age' in which a benevolent monarch presided over an increasingly prosperous nation, but this is not a true picture. Portrayals of the 'good outlaw' in popular culture, barring a few printed copies of the *Gest* and of other outlaw tales such as *Adam Bell, Clim of Clough,* and *William of Cloudeslie*, were becoming fewer and fewer. At the same time there was an intense fear of normal, everyday criminals, especially in London, who were collectively labeled 'rogues', a term first coined in John Awdley's *Fraternity of Vagabonds* (1561). More menacing and nastier than the outlaw, these fellows were indistinguishable from law-abiding citizens. They knew no moral code, like the greenwood thieves of old did; instead they stole from people, both men and women, rich and poor, indiscriminately. They were described as 'masterless men', loyal to nobody. Clearly, common thieves were being idealised to a lesser extent in the sixteenth century. By the 1590s, there was a flurry of literature which aimed to shine a light on the menacing creatures who inhabited this emerging underworld, many of which in this decade were authored by Robert Greene, such as *A Notable Discovery of Cozenage* (1591); Greene's *The Black Book's Messenger* (1592); *Third and Last Part of Cony-Catching* (1592); *The Defence of Cony-Catching* (1592); *A Disputation between a Hee Conny-Cathcer and a Shee Conny-Cathcer* (1592). It cannot be a coincidence, therefore, that in the same decade that there was increasing anxiety regarding crime in the capital, the London-based Munday 'gentrifies' England's most famous thief, making him, in popular culture, 'the most humane and the prince of all robbers'.

Munday is clearly trying to maintain Robin Hood's 'good outlaw' image which is why he portrays him as noble, both in character and rank. One thing about rogue literature is the fact that the rogues in them are not always law-breakers. Often they resort to trickery and embezzlement while keeping technically within the law. Thus, the rogues in Munday's play are people like Warman, Robin's betrayer and the future Sheriff of Nottingham; due to the underhand methods of rogues, who aimed to advance in society, not through plain thievery but through cunning and intrigue, in Munday's play it is Warman, Robin's betrayer and the future Sheriff of Nottingham.

Let it be remembered also, that in the earlier Robin Hood poems Robin was a simple yeoman. In the mid-sixteenth century, some members of the yeoman class, along with husbandmen, labourers, and craftsmen, had also been rather unruly, having instigated riots against common land enclosures. The more immediate context of Munday's stories is the fact that when he was writing the plays, for almost a decade London had been plagued by a series of riots due to a number of factors. England's economy was still primarily an agricultural one at that point, in spite of its budding overseas trading interests. Four successive harvests failed between 1593 and 1597, which led to food shortages and high prices for staple goods; prices for flour alone are said to have increased by 190 per cent. Falling wages, unemployment, as well as the continuing enclosures of common lands, further compounded contemporary social and economic problems and, naturally, people blamed the government. As ever, the worst hardships were felt by those at the bottom of the social hierarchy, in particular apprentices, and these young lads instigated a series of riots between 1590 and 1595. The government was so worried that it issued a Royal Proclamation in 1590 calling for curfews to be applied to apprentices. The most notorious of these apprentice riots occurred in 1595, when 1,000 apprentices marched on Tower Hill to protest appalling working conditions. While the rebellion was put down, the protestors were charged not with minor public order offences but with treason.

In spite of Henry VIII having played Robin Hood, the outlaw – as a provincial folk figure – was a riotous figure in early modern May Day games, often twinned with the personification of the 'Lord of Misrule', and some of the games did on occasion spill over into outright riots, as illustrated by the May Day Riots (1517). The early Robin Hood texts also contain hints of limited forms of social protest, such as an expression of grievances against pavage, and at the end of the *Gest*, which was in print when Munday was writing, Robin does defy the king and return to live in the greenwood. At a time when criminals are becoming ever more threatening, when yeoman, from which the 'original' Robin Hood of the ballads hailed, are guilty of defying the established order, perhaps there was a need for Robin Hood, who was gradually acquiring the status of a national hero, to undergo a conservatising process and become an establishment figure. He does not defy the wishes of Richard I at the end but instead stays loyal to the monarch throughout.

There is no evidence to suggest that Munday's plays reached a wide audience. This is due to the fact that they were performed only once in 1599. It is more likely that people acquired their understanding of Robin Hood as an earl from a popular ballad that was published a little later during the seventeenth century entitled *A True Tale of Robin Hood* (1631). Ballads were published on broadsides, single sheets of paper with printed song lyrics on them and sold by street sellers often for a penny or less. Such was their popularity that broadsides were being sold right up until the end of the nineteenth century. Often the ballads were badly written and it was not without some justification that, in the eighteenth century, many street ballads were derided as being 'the refuse of a stall'. The upper classes had varying views of the ballad, often seeing them as a diversion for the vulgar part of society who liked to celebrate the lives and misdeeds of notorious criminals, as illustrated in the following poem which appeared in *The Universal Magazine* in 1760:

> With hideous face and tuneless note,
> The ballad-singer strains his throat;
> Roars out the life of Betty Saunders,
> With Turpin Dick and Molly Flanders.
> Tells many woeful tragic stories,
> Recorded of our British worthies.
> Forgetting not Bold Robin Hood,
> And hardy Scarlet of the Wood.

Alternatively, some people from higher stations of life loved 'folk' ballads. In an issue of Joseph Addison's *Spectator* magazine from 1711, he writes with fondness of the ballad of *The Two Children in the Wood*, 'which has been the delight of most Englishmen in some part of their age'. In a very odd turn, the story of *The Two Children in the Wood* was merged with that of Robin Hood in nineteenth-century pantomimes. In the traditional story, two children are murdered by their wicked uncle. In the Victorian version, however, they are saved by Robin Hood and Maid Marian. The *Robin Hood and the Babes in Wood* pantomime is performed to this day in many variety theatres in the United Kingdom.

Many early modern ballads only survived to the present day, in fact, because members of the upper classes collected and preserved them for posterity. The famous diarist, Samuel Pepys (1633–1703), collected 1,800 broadside ballads which now form the bulk of the Pepys Collection, housed at Magdalene College, Cambridge. Robert Harley, 1st Earl of Oxford and Mortimer (1661–1724), along with John Ker, 3rd Duke of Roxburghe, collected what is now the collection known as Roxburghe Ballads (1740–1804). The fact that such distinguished men collected these, as well as Addison's comments above, gives credence to Peter Burke's theory about the often invisible distinctions between high culture and popular culture in the early modern period. Anthologies of ballads also often appeared in books known as 'garlands'. These were collections of songs arranged around a particular theme. While broadsides were ephemeral and easily lost or damaged, copies of *Robin Hood's Garland*, which, marketed towards the bourgeoisie and retailing at a few shillings, were significantly more expensive than broadsides. Being more durable and less ephemeral than the average broadside, garlands became important source texts for later historians carrying out research into the legend of Robin Hood. Ballads were not only the songs of the common people who hummed them as they toiled away in the fields, for people of all classes enjoyed listening to ballads, in spite of what many Victorian historians thought.

Most of the ballads published throughout the seventeenth century were written anonymously and are often of poor literary merit, although they are nonetheless enjoyable to listen to. We do know who the author of the *True Tale* was: Martin Parker (c. 1600–c. 1656). Although we know very little of Parker's early life, he turned his hand to a number of subjects and turned them into songs for people's enjoyment such as *The Tale of Tom Thumb*, *Arthur King of the Britains* [sic], *The History of St George*, which were often set to contemporary popular melodies. All classes enjoyed such songs, and Parker's *True Tale* addresses a socially diverse readership and alerts them to Robin Hood's new-found aristocratic status:

> Both gentlemen, or yeomen bould,
> Or whatsoever you are,
> To have a stately story tould,
> Attention now prepare …

> This Robin so much talked on,
> Was once a man of fame,
> Instiled Earle of Huntington,
> Lord Robert Hood by name.

It is then said that Robin Hood, in typical aristocratic fashion, squandered his wealth and ended up in debt, which is the reason he took flight into the forest to live as an outlaw. He was not a cut-throat, however, for he never harms women and after he dies towards the end of the ballad, Parker prints a copy of the epitaph which supposedly appeared on Robin Hood's grave:

> Robert Earle of Huntington
> Lies under this little stone,
> No archer was like him so good;
> His wildness named him Robbin Hood.
> Full thirteen years and somewhat more,
> These northern parts he vexed sore,
> Such outlaws as he and his men,
> May England never know again.

A hackneyed version of this epitaph, written in faux-Middle English, can be seen on Robin Hood's alleged grave in Kirklees to this day. Obviously this epitaph, which may even have been invented by Parker, has nothing to do with any 'real' Robin Hood, for he was never originally depicted as a nobleman in any early text or court roll. At any rate, while Munday initiated the storyline that Robin Hood was a dispossessed earl, it is likely Parker's ballad, which had the potential of being read by a wide audience and was reprinted several times in broadside and pamphlet form during the seventeenth and eighteenth centuries, that was responsible for the dissemination of the idea.

Many more Robin Hood ballads appeared throughout the century as writers sought to capitalise upon the existing popularity of outlaw tales. Some of the ballads which are published in this period often depict Robin Hood as little more than a buffoon in Robin-Hood-meets-his-match scenarios. The ballad of *Robin Hood and the Tanner* is one example of this. Robin sees a tanner named Arthur travelling through the forest; Robin decides that he wants some 'sport' with the tanner so Robin pretends to be the king's forester and bids Arthur to stop. Arthur simply laughs at the fact that Robin is alone, to which Robin threatens to get out his 'staff of another oake graffe' with which to fight him. A fight with quarterstaffs ensues and Robin loses badly:

> Then Arthur soon he recovered himself
> And he gave [Robin] a knock on the crown,
> That on every hair of bold Robin Hood's head,
> The blood came trickling down.

Robin calls for quarter and, so impressed with his toughness, asks whether Arthur will join his band of outlaws:

> But if thou'lt forsake thy tanners trade
> And live in green wood with me,

ROBIN HOOD

> My name's Robin Hood and I swear by the rood,
> I will give thee both gold and fee.

There are also some heroic portrayals of Robin Hood featured on broadside ballads. The ballad of *Robin Hood and the Three Squires*, a variation of which is sometimes titled *Robin Hood Rescuing the Widow's Three Sons*, sees Robin encountering a distraught old lady in the forest. She is upset because her sons are due to be hanged by the sheriff in Nottingham. What is interesting about one of the surviving versions of this text is that Robin ensures the widow's sons are deserving of being rescued first before he decides to do anything about their predicament:

> 'What news? What news, thou silly old woman?
> What news hast thou for me?'
> Said she, 'There's three squires in Nottingham town
> Today is condemned to die.'
>
> 'O have they parishes burnt?' he said,
> 'Or have they ministers slain?
> Or have they robbed any virgin,
> Or with other men's wives lain?'

Clearly, Robin Hood is reasonable and is not opposed to every punishment the sheriff carries out in the maintenance of law and order. However, it turns out that they are being hanged because they have killed the king's deer so Robin's sympathies lay with them and he resolves to save them from the noose. In disguise, he goes to Nottingham and volunteers to be the hangman. Just before the men are about to be hanged Robin blows on his horn and over a hundred of his men come riding over the hill, a scene which would be captured brilliantly by the engraver John Bewick (1760–95). They set the men free and then capture the sheriff and take him back to the glen, where they build a gallows from which they hang the sheriff.

Although many writers throughout history have dressed Robin and his men up as noble criminals, the merry men are essentially an organised crime network. Whoever wrote *Robin Hood Rescuing the Widow's Three Sons* has a rudimentary understanding of the political economy of organised crime, and its relationship with the state and law enforcement. Throughout history, organised criminal gangs are content to not cause too much trouble for local law enforcement. In fact, laying low and not bothering law enforcement in their daily duties is often beneficial for bands of criminals: it takes the heat away from them. The merry men need to be seen as the 'good guys'; they depend, as all bandits do, upon the goodwill and favour of the people; not a single soul would look favourably upon Robin and his men if they were to rescue from the gallows arsonists, adulterers, or those who mistreated women.

It is tempting to think that the arrival of print culture immediately displaced an older oral and manuscript culture. But it should not be forgotten that there was also a flourishing manuscript culture well into the eighteenth century. People often wrote down, for their own private use, various poems and songs that they had heard perhaps at work, in the streets, or at festivals. Sometimes they would ask friends and relatives to send them new verses. After all, books would have been expensive for many people, even for those from middle stations of life. Women, in particular, often kept personalised collections of verse and song. On 31 July 1638, for example, a woman named Constance Fowler wrote to her brother asking him to send her some pieces of verse so that she could copy them and put them in her 'booke'. Around 1703, a Shropshire gentleman by the name of Sir John Bridgeman likewise compiled a 'manuscript miscellany' of verse, among which was a copy of a play by the infamous Earl of Rochester (1647–80). The prevalence of this practice is further evident in the existence of the *Forresters Manuscript* (or to give the manuscript its official title, British Library, MS Additional 71158). It was discovered in 1992, and it is a collection of twenty-four early modern Robin Hood ballads. Two people contributed to its compilation judging by the differences in handwriting that can be discerned from a physical study of the manuscript. Of course, the people who were copying these down for private use had no need to sensationalise the ballads' titles to make a profit, unlike the broadside publishers. As Stephen Knight points out, the titles of some of them are amended to sound rather more modest. What was *The Noble Fisherman* for a broadside title was modified to *Robin Hood's Fishing*; the same story that is listed as *Robin Hood Newly Reviv'd* on broadside ballads is listed simply as *Robin Hood and the Stranger* in the manuscript.

Moving on from ballads, we now come to examine the work of one of the early modern period's most celebrated dramatists, Ben Jonson (1572–1637). He authored a rather unique portrayal of the Robin Hood story entitled *The Sad Shepherd; or A Tale of Robin Hood*, which was left unfinished before his death in 1637. It is a pastoral play, and these works depict an idealised vision of rural life. They often feature, as their main protagonists, simple country folk such as shepherds and shepherdesses. Jonson wrote a variety of plays and masques for a predominantly courtly, aristocratic audience. He reached the height of his success after the accession of James I (1566–1625). Throughout his career, he avoided writing historical dramas and instead preferred to write satires and comedies. His most famous and well-regarded works were *Everyman in his Humour* (1598), *Volpone* (1605), *Bartholomew Fair* (1614). Jonson's style was different to that of some of his contemporaries, known as the Spenserians, who looked back with a nostalgic fondness on the Elizabethan period. Spenserians were so named because they wrote in the style of Edmund Spenser, the author of the long narrative poem, *The Faerie Queene* (1590–96). As Jonson grew older, however, he began to experiment with more archaic styles of writing, such as the pastoral.

In Jonson's play, it is unclear whether Robin Hood is an outlaw or not, and his designation is 'the Chief Woodsman and Master of the Feast'. If we assume that sixteenth-century writers were indeed making Robin Hood conservative, or gentrified, according to Stephen Knight, then it makes sense to see Robin in this play not as a criminal but as a merely rustic woodland inhabitant. The setting is Sherwood Forest, which when Jonson was writing was more or less widely regarded as the undisputed home of Robin Hood and his men. It is a very peaceful Sherwood with very little danger, at least to begin with; Robin Hood has invited all of the shepherds and shepherdesses to a feast. However, this idyll is interrupted when one of the shepherds, Aeglamour, is distraught because his true love, Earine, has reportedly drowned in the River Trent (hence 'the sad shepherd'). Robin Hood and company attempt to comfort him but he is too distraught, so Robin leaves him to go and see Marian where each one confesses their mutual love for each other. Later on, Marian leads all of the shepherdesses into 'Robin Hood's kitchen'. She quarrels with Robin Hood, takes the venison, and storms out, thus leaving everyone confused. It turns out that the bad witch, Maudlin 'the Envious', has impersonated Marian in order to begin a quarrel with Robin Hood and sow divisions among the close-knit community. Maudlin is also responsible for Aeglamour's sorrow because she has kidnapped Aeglamour's lover, Earine, and stripped her of all her clothes because she was envious of the girl's fine posessions. Robin eventually wises up to Maudlin and her children's schemes and so sends men to apprehend her, which is where the play finishes.

The story is essentially one about the clash of values; the small society of Robin Hood and his men is based upon a collective good, whereas Maudlin and her children are motivated by greed, self-interest and pride. As to how Jonson would have finished the play, no one can be sure. There is a possibility that in the end the forest would return to harmony and even Maudlin and her children would be invited to the banquet of venison at the end. This is because, as Ann Barton points out, one character listed in the dramatis personae is one Reuben 'the Reconciler'. Although Reuben does not speak in the fragment that Jonson completed, Jonson's characters' names often designated the function that they served so he must have intended Reuben to have had a purpose.

The play has never been performed and very rarely did new plays, even those which were performed in the late-Elizabethan or Jacobean eras, get printed immediately. Dramatists aimed to see their works played on the stage, and were not as invested in seeing their works in print. The attitude of many contemporary dramatists towards seeing their works in print, in fact, is encapsulated in the words of John Marston (1576–1634) who said that 'only one thing afflicts me, to think that scenes, invented merely to be spoken, should be enforcively published to read'. When a production company agreed to purchase a play from a dramatist, they often ordered only a few copies of it for the players, although this did not prevent some booksellers from printing a few additional pirated versions of the plays to sell to readers. Many of these printings of individual plays, known as 'quartos' were ephemeral and do not survive. This does not mean, however, that plays did not reach the wider reading public during the seventeenth century. Long after the plays had ceased their run on the stage, publishers took it upon themselves to produce collections of dramatists' works in folios, which were large books containing all of a playwright's plays. Ben Jonson's First Folio was published in 1616, before he wrote *The Sad Shepherd*, and contained his most famous plays. The publication of his plays took Jonson's plays out of the realm of ephemera and into high literature. The printing of these plays in such a format seems to have been the inspiration behind the publication of Shakespeare's First Folio in 1623. It is in Jonson's Second Folio, published in 1641, that *The Sad Shepherd* first made its appearance as a work of literature for an audience of fairly affluent readers and book collectors. The most popular and accessible edition of Jonson's play, however, was published with a continuation, notes, and an appendix by Francis Waldron in 1783, which was part of the emerging antiquarian interest in English history during the late eighteenth century.

While the late sixteenth and early seventeenth centuries witnessed a boom in English literature, the mid-seventeenth century was a turbulent time, for England experienced its first revolution led by General Thomas Fairfax (1612–71) and Oliver Cromwell (1599–1658). There had of course been serious revolts before in English history, such as the so-called Peasants' Revolt of 1381. But Wat Tyler, John Ball, Jack Straw, and the rebels back then never wanted to abolish the monarchy, or so they claimed at any rate. Instead it was under Cromwell that the first serious challenge to kingly authority from the people was mounted.

King Charles I ascended the thrones of England, Scotland, and Ireland in 1625. From the beginning of his reign he made a series of mistakes that alienated not only the parliamentary ruling class, but a significant number of the people at large. In 1626, when parliamentarians were unhappy with one of his advisors, George Villiers, and asked that he be dismissed from office, Charles, viewing this as an affront to his authority, dismissed Parliament. Charles was forced to call Parliament back again later when he needed money to finance a war, but the relationship between king and Parliament was on the rocks. Another of his blunders was to demand Ship Tax from people; it was previously a tax which the monarch could levy on the inhabitants of coastal towns and it did not require the consent of Parliament. Charles, however, attempted to enforce it upon tax payers living in inland parts of the country as well. Some MPs drew up the Petition of Right which, in one of its articles, said that any merchant who paid any 'illegal' tax which had not been authorised by Parliament was a traitor to England. Charles had some of the MPs responsible for drawing up this charter arrested, which further alienated him from the very people with whom he was supposed to be working to govern the country. Exasperated with Parliament for not bending to his will, in 1629, he commenced an eleven-year period of personal rule during which he governed with the use of the Royal Prerogative. It was Charles's attempted arrest of five MPs in 1642 which brought the country to the brink of war; Parliament refused to recognise the charge and, as a result, Charles raised his standard against Parliament.

The result of the English Revolution is well known. Charles's armies eventually lost and the king was placed on trial for treason, found guilty, and beheaded. Oliver Cromwell then established the Commonwealth of England which lasted from 1649 until 1660. By all accounts, it was quite an austere experience living under the puritan republican dictator. Theatres were closed in 1642, and playwrights and theatre managers could be fined if it was found they had staged a play. As an environment, the theatre was associated with irreligiosity and debauchery, and was deemed to be at odds with godly puritan ideology. The ban was not wholly effective, however, and a further ban on theatres had to be passed in 1648. Christmas in this period, contrary to what some might believe, was not banned, but the Cromwellian Parliament did insist that it should cease to be a time of overindulgence and mirth but should, as a public holiday, be kept as a sombre reminder of the Lord's birth. After Cromwell's death, his son Richard was briefly installed as Lord Protector but he was clearly not up to the task as he lacked the support of the army. England needed a ruler and so Charles Stuart, the son of Charles II, agreed to return to England and take up the throne. He commenced his reign in May 1660.

Known as the 'merry monarch', the theatres reopened and it seemed that people could enjoy themselves again. Charles II was fond of music, theatre, and also liked his women. He was everything that Cromwell was not. We see Robin Hood briefly appear on stage again during the Restoration in a short play entitled *Robin Hood and his Crew of Souldiers*, which was 'acted at Nottingham on the day of His Sacred Majesties Corronation' in 1660, the text of which was published a year later. Nottingham by this time had been firmly established in popular consciousness as the place where Robin Hood had allegedly carried out his exploits. In the play, Robin Hood and his men, having for a period of time been unruly and disobedient to the king, are reconciled to him at the end and agree to be his servants. The opening passage is clearly meant to reflect the sense of optimism that greeted the arrival of a new king in the 1660s:

Enter Hobin [sic] Hood, little John, William Scadlock, &c.

Whence springs this general joy?
What means this noise that makes Heavens
Arch'd vault echo?

… Tis the Kings Coronation; and now the Shieriffe with a
band of men, are marching to reduce us to loyalty.

The sheriff's messenger eventually persuades the outlaws to swear loyalty to the new king because he offers all those who were previously opposed to him a pardon:

This Great, this Gracious Prince is this day crown'd, and offers
Life, and Peace, and Honour, if you will quit your wilde rebellions,
and become what your birth challenges of you, (nay what ever
your boasted gallanty expects of you that is) loyall subjects.

ROBIN HOOD

The play speaks of Robin Hood and his men as having committed vaguely defined 'crimes'. This can be read as crimes against the government, and not simply petty theft or highway robbery as modern audiences might expect. Robin Hood had served as an anti-government figure in the earlier part of the century, when the men involved in the Gunpowder Plot in 1605 were described as 'Robin Hoods'. So it was not unusual to see Robin Hood and his men depicted as semi-revolutionaries in this period, although their dangerous tendencies are nicely contained in this play. The merry men, furthermore, are not outlaws in this play but soldiers, and the sight on stage of a king's messenger urging soldiers to lay down their arms and support a new king would have had resonance for people seeing it in 1661. It is evident that these formerly rebellious men have learned the errors of their ways and decided to welcome the new king. While Charles II did experience some opposition from certain sections of Cromwell's New Model Army, some of the regiments after 1661 were, as a result of their services in ensuring the continuation of law and order in the capital, incorporated into the new royal army. Then at the end of the play, Robin and his soldiers break out into a sycophantic song expressing their love for the new king:

> Let us all then joyne in the present sence of our duty, accept the profer'd pardon, – and with one voice sing, with hearty Wishes, health unto our King.

> Since Heaven with a liberal hand,
> Doth choicest blessings fling,
> And hath (not only to our Land
> Restor'd but) Crown'd our KING.

> Let us to joy and generall mirth
> This glad day set aside,
> Let the Neighb'ring Woods now Eccho forth,
> Our shouts and Loyal Pride.

> May Halters that Mans fate attend
> That envies this dayes Glee
> And's name meet a perpetual brand
> For his Disloyalty.

Now all was to be forgiven. Yet clearly there was a veiled warning to those who would shun the king's good grace: a halter would be placed around traitors' necks and they would be forever branded as an enemy of the king. Whoever the author of this play was, they were clearly supportive of the new monarch.

In this era of ballads and plays, shortly after the English Revolution, we also see the emergence of the first fictional prose narratives of Robin Hood. One of the earliest surviving prose accounts of Robin Hood is the 'Sloane Life of Robin Hood' manuscript (c. 1600), which relates to our earlier point about the persistence of manuscript culture well after the arrival of the printing press. Without any historical precedent, this manuscript was the first to state that Robin Hood 'was borne at Lockesley in Yorkeshyre'. The addition of the Locksley birthplace in this text was probably contained in a poem or ballad that is now lost to us. The now anonymous author is evidently acquainted with printed versions of the *Gest* for reference is made to Sir Richard of the Lee and the £400 debt to the Abbot of St Mary's. Later in the seventeenth century, however, Robin's first appearance in published prose fiction would be marked with the publication of *The Noble Birth and Gallant Atchievements of that Remarkable Out-Law Robin Hood* (1678).

In the sixteenth century a peculiar genre of romance emerged known as picaresque fiction. It originated in Spain and portrayed the lives of rogues and criminals. The first such Spanish work was entitled *Lazarillo de Tormes* (1554). Works were translated into English such as James Mabbe's *Guzman de Alfarache* (1622). Later in the seventeenth century was the famous work *The English Rogue* (1665) which, in the words of Hal Gladfelder, marked the genre's full assimilation into English. *The Noble Birth and Gallant Atchievements of that Remarkable Out-Law Robin Hood* (1662) is significant because it appears to be an attempt to situate stories of England's most famous outlaw within the genre of English rogue fiction. It is not known who the author of *The Noble Birth* was, other than that he was, 'an Ingenious Antiquary' who had collected all of the different materials purporting to tell the details of Robin Hood's life. The authors of English rogue fiction had to somehow claim authority on a subject. Writers often pretended that their stories were either from the mouths of real criminals, or collected from a criminal's memoirs and private papers which had fallen into their hands. Richard Head followed this practice in the preface to *Jackson's Recantation* (1674), an early criminal biography, in which he declared that:

> Reader, let me assure thee this is no fiction, but a true relation
> of Mr. Jacksons life and conversation, Pen'd by his own

hand, and delivered into mine to be made publick for his Countrymens good, in compensation of the many injuries he hath done them.

This was a practice which continued in criminal biographies in the eighteenth century, as well as later novels. Daniel Defoe's *Moll Flanders* (1722), for example, claims to have been 'written from her own memorandums'. The author of *The Noble Birth* is similarly attempting the same with Robin Hood; given the fact that Robin is not a contemporary seventeenth-century figure, however, the author claimed an authority on the subject through presenting himself as the ingenious antiquary who has researched the subject thoroughly and is presenting the facts.

As the title implies, the author states that Robin was born the heir to the Earl of Huntingdon's estate. But to the antiquary, the fact that Robin was of noble birth does not automatically mean that the outlaw was upright and moral at the beginning of his life. He tells us that Robin was 'outlaw'd by Henry the Eight for many extravagances and outrages he committed, [and] did draw together a company of such bold and licentious persons as himself'. We are not told why Robin turns to a life of crime, merely that he was 'bold and licentious'. There are no lofty ideals which make him take to a life in the greenwood. Rather, like many protagonists in seventeenth-century rogue fiction, Robin acts in his own self-interest. Robin's actions are thus reflective of the emergent ideology of bourgeois individualism in the seventeenth century. The stories that follow the introduction to Robin Hood's life are taken directly from many of the later seventeenth-century ballads such as *Robin Hood's Delight, Robin Hood's Progress to Nottingham, Robin Hood and the Tanner, Robin Hood and the Curtall Friar*, and *Robin Hood's Chase*. As with all seventeenth-century criminal narratives, the action moves at a rapid pace. Rarely does the author expend more than two pages detailing the events of each ballad. This is another feature of English rogue fiction: the incidents that they relate in the rogue's life are short and episodic, move at a rapid pace, and the world that the rogue inhabits is characterised by chance meetings and clashes with other individuals. Adapting the later Robin Hood ballads to this end therefore works well for the author of *The Noble Birth* here, as in the ballads, Robin does indeed meet with a number of people from various social classes. The rapidity of narration would be emulated in later criminal biographies during the eighteenth century, and Alexander Smith's entry on Robin Hood in his *A Complete History of the Lives and Robberies of the Most Notorious Highwaymen* (1719), and Charles Johnson's *Lives and Exploits of the Most Noted Highwaymen* (1734) owe a lot to the author of *The Noble Birth*. The major departure which *The Noble Birth* makes from the Robin Hood tradition is in its account of the outlaw's later life. As we have seen, in *A Gest of Robyn Hode*, he is bled to death by the Prioress of Kirklees who conspires with her lover, Sir Roger of Doncaster, to kill Robin. And it is a story that is usually repeated in the oft-reprinted garland versions of the ballad of *Robin Hood's Death and Burial*, as well as in Smith and Johnson's eighteenth-century narratives. But in this story we are told that:

> He spent his old age in peace, at a house of his own, not far from Nottingham, being generally beloved and respected of all … Robin Hood dismissed all his idle companions, and betaking himself to a civil course of life, he did keep a gallant house, and had over all the country, the love of the rich, and the prayers of the poor.

The penitence in Robin Hood's later life is another feature of *The Noble Birth* which marks it out as an example of rogue fiction. Robin Hood may have been a man of dubious moral standing at the beginning of the story, but by the end he has reformed himself. Other examples of rogue fiction present similar endings with statements. For example, Robert Greene's *The Conversion of an English Courtezan* (1592) indicates that the harlot has laid aside her vicious course of life by saying that, 'I have set downe at the end of my disputation, the wonderful life of a curtezin, not a fiction, but a truth of one that yet liues, not now in an other forme repentant'. *The Noble Birth*, of course, is not a historicist's interpretation of the medieval period. There are no grand knights in shining armour or big castles featured in the text. In fact, Robin is not a medieval figure at all in *The Noble Birth*, but instead is said to have lived in the early modern period during the days of Henry VIII. This is perhaps an indication that the ingenious antiquary got confused when reading of Munday's play, whose framing narrative is set during the time of Henry VIII. Despite the fact that the author claims to be 'an ingenious antiquary', he pays little regard to looking for historical accuracy. Despite being of little value to those who would seek to find a 'real' Robin Hood, this work is significant as it is one of the first appearances of Robin Hood in an English mass-market prose narrative. It is further evidence of the fact that, by the seventeenth century, the Robin Hood tradition is moving from being a predominantly oral tradition to a textual one. Previously Robin's story had been told in ballads, poems, and Latin chronicles, but this work marks the assimilation of Robin Hood into the English literary sphere.

One of the earliest images of Robin Hood which appeared on the front cover of an early edition of *A Gest of Robyn Hode*, printed in Antwerp between c. 1510 and c. 1515.

Robin Hood and Little John in the Greenwood, as illustrated by John Bewick.

A disguised Robin Hood dines with the Sheriff of Nottingham.

Robin Hood's battle with Guy of Gisborne.

Robin Hood and his merry men.

Robin Hood's first meeting with Clorinda, 'the Queen of the Shepherdesses'.

Allen-a-Dale plays a song for the merry men.

Robin Hood killing the fifteen foresters.

Robin Hood fights with George-a-Green, the Pindar of Wakefield.

Robin Hood waylays a bishop.

Robin Hood meets the butcher in the forest.

A lonely deer in the greenwood.

Robin Hood's fight with the tanner, Arthur-a-Bland.

Robin Hood meets the tinker.

Robin Hood disguised as a musician.

Robin Hood sets his sights on a deer.

Robin Hood asleep in the greenwood.

The Curtal Friar carries Robin on his back through the water.

Robin Hood fights a stranger.

Robin Hood
shooting in an
archery contest
in front of the
king and queen.

The king and
Robin Hood on
horseback.

Robin Hood
and his men
disguised as
monks.

Robin Hood rescues the widow's three sons from the gallows.

The battle of the English and French ships from *The Noble Fisherman*.

The merry men fight each other before making friends and banding together.

Robin Hood meets a poor beggar.

Above: Little John and the four beggars.

Left: Little John's first meeting with Robin Hood.

Above left: Little John in the Sheriff of Nottingham's kitchen.

Above right: The Prioress of Kirklees leads Robin Hood to his death.

Right: The merry men bind the Bishop of Hereford to a tree.

Left: An early modern image of George-a-Green.

Below: A seventeenth-century woodcut of Robin Hood, Little John and Will Scarlet.

ROBIN HOOD:

A

COLLECTION

OF ALL THE ANCIENT

POEMS, SONGS, AND BALLADS,

NOW EXTANT,

RELATIVE TO THAT CELEBRATED

ENGLISH OUTLAW:

TO WHICH ARE PREFIXED

HISTORICAL ANECDOTES OF HIS LIFE.

IN TWO VOLUMES.

VOLUME THE FIRST.

In this our fpacious ifle I think there is not one,
But he ' of ROBIN HOOD hath beard' and Little John;
And to the end of time the tales fhall ne'er be done
Of Scarlock, George a Green, and Much the miller's fon,
Of Tuck, the merry friar, which many a fermon made
In praife of ROBIN HOOD, his out-laws, and their trade.

DRAYTON.

LONDON:

PRINTED FOR T. EGERTON, WHITEHALL, AND
J. JOHNSON, ST. PAULS-CHURCH-YARD.

MDCCXCV.

Title page to Joseph Ritson's *Robin Hood* (1795).

A Victorian depiction of Friar Tuck.

Sir Walter Scott, the author of *Ivanhoe* (1819).

Pierce Egan the Younger, the author of *Robin Hood and Little John* (1838–40).

Thomas Percy, editor of *Reliques of Ancient English Poetry* (1765).

The eccentric Joseph Ritson, editor of *Robin Hood: A Collection of All the Ancient Poems, Songs, and Ballads* (1795).

Thomas Love Peacock, author of *Maid Marian* (1822).

Right: Robert Southey, author of *Harold; or the Castle of Morford* (1791).

Below: Herne the Hunter, as depicted in William Harrison Ainsworth's *Windsor Castle* (1842).

Left: Robin Hood meeting the Forest Demon, from George Emmett's *Robin Hood* (1869).

Below: Conisbrough Castle as illustrated in a late-Victorian edition of *Ivanhoe*.

Robin Hood and
Maid Marian.

Robin Hood meets the beggar,
from Henry Gilbert's *Robin
Hood* (1912).

Robin Hood · meeteth · the · tall
Stranger · on · the · Bridge

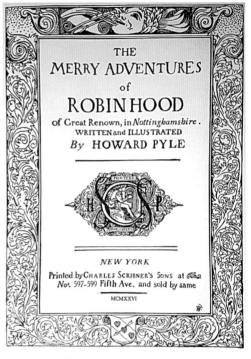

THE
MERRY ADVENTURES
of
ROBIN HOOD
of Great Renown, in *Nottinghamshire*.
WRITTEN and ILLUSTRATED
By HOWARD PYLE

NEW YORK
Printed by CHARLES SCRIBNER'S SONS at
Nos. 597-599 Fifth Ave, and sold by same
MCMXXVI

Above left: Howard Pyle's illustration of Robin Hood meeting with a stranger.

Above right: Title page to Howard Pyle's *Merry Adventures of Robin Hood* (1883).

Left: Robin Hood makes a daring escape from Nottingham Castle.

Title page to George Emmett's
Robin Hood.

A feast at Gamwell
Hall, as illustrated
by Pierce Egan the
Younger.

Above: Nottingham Castle in the eighteenth century.

Below left: First edition of Pierce Egan's *Robin Hood*.

Below right: Title page to the revised edition of Pierce Egan's *Robin Hood*.

Chapter 4

The Eighteenth Century

The Trump of fame your name has breath'd
Its praise is sounded far and near;
Stout Little John with laurel wreath'd
Has reeach'd each dame and damsel's ear;
But 'tis not you but Bold Robin Hood,
I come to seek with bended bow;
That man of might,
I fain would fight,
And conquer with my – Oh, oh, oh!

The Sherwood Songster (1783)

The eighteenth century is generally considered to be an age in which neoclassicism dominated the arts scene. The works of major literary figures, such as John Dryden (1631–1700), Joseph Addison (1672–1719), Richard Steele (1672–1729), Alexander Pope (1688–1744), and Henry Fielding (1702–1754) were influenced by their education in classical literature and history. Much of this enthusiasm for all things Greek and Roman was facilitated by the spread of print culture which enabled people to access ancient texts that had previously, by and large, been available only to learned people in universities or connected with the church. Dryden's efforts in translating some historical texts into English, such as Ovid's *Metamorphoses*, for the aspirational and increasingly important bourgeoisie, meant that those who lacked a formal education could enjoy these texts. Through the cultivation of such 'polite arts', such readers could be admitted into polite society.

However, the enthusiasm for all things classical among elite writers did not mean that there was a denigration of England's medieval heritage, even if portrayals of the medieval past were often given a baroque or neoclassical overlay. Thomas Arne's opera *Alfred* (1740), which tells the story of England's historical warrior king, was immensely popular and is perhaps best known for the song played in its finale entitled *Rule Britannia*. In an essay for the *Tatler*, published in 1711, Addison declares that Robin Hood is a 'British worthy', a man whose achievements surpass those of other medieval heroes and who can be reckoned as a great hero in a similar manner to Achilles or Julius Caesar.

Dryden had a high degree of interest in England's medieval past. He wrote the highly successful play *King Arthur; or, The British Worthy* in 1691, which was accompanied with an elegant musical score by the composer Henry Purcell (1659–95). Dryden also translated some of the works of Chaucer in his *Fables: Ancient and Modern* (1700). But Dryden also kept an eye on the popular culture of the day, and to this end, in partnership with his friend, the printer Jacob Tonson, he published several volumes of *Miscellany Poems* which appeared between 1684 and 1694. These volumes were reprinted frequently. The sixth volume was published after Dryden's death in 1700, and it is in this book that *A Ballad of Bold Robin Hood, Shewing his Birth, Breeding, and Valour* was, for example, reprinted for a polite, middle-class audience.

The medieval *Gest of Robyn Hode* seems to have been forgotten about in the late seventeenth and early eighteenth centuries. *A Ballad of Bold Robin Hood, Shewing his Birth, Breeding, and Valour*, therefore, was the only popular song available which provided Robin Hood with a biography. It was republished in some editions of *Robin Hood's Garland*, and then again in several expensive multivolume collections of ballads. This song completely ignores the idea that Robin was an aristocrat and he is instead depicted as the son of a humble forester. His mother is the niece of a gentleman named Gamwell, and she takes Robin Hood to Gamwell Hall to spend Christmas with the extended family. It is here that Robin is introduced to Little John. The ballad is unclear on the point of whether Robin Hood is an outlaw or not. Doubtless contemporary readers would have immediately thought of Robin as a thief, but this is not communicated with any clarity in the story itself. Robin then meets a woman named Clorinda. She is a rather simple peasant girl, named the 'Queen of the Shepherdesses' in some of the subtitles given to this song in its later editions. The visionary artist and poet, William Blake, depicted Robin and Clordinda's marriage in a print entitled *Robin Hood and Clorinda* (1783). The pair exchange sweet words, she kills a deer, after which Robin briefly gets into a fight with some forest yeomen. At the end of the ballad Robin and Clorinda are married. Clearly, even in spite of Marian's appearance in May Games and Munday's *Huntingdon* plays, her position as Robin Hood's sweetheart was not yet cemented in popular culture.

Another 'miscellany' poem that was possibly written by John Winstanley was published in *Poems Written on Several Occasions* (1742).

Classicism had seeped into eighteenth-century portrayals of the Middle Ages, and in Winstanley's Robin Hood poems we see the outlaw challenging Apollo to an archery match, although the challenges, in keeping with eighteenth-century polite etiquette, are issued as invitations:

'An Invitation to Robin Hood'

SIR, *Thursday* next, the *Archers* dine,
On *Round* of beef, if not Sir Loin;
Though *Round* suits best, at *B—r's* House,
A Glass to drink, and to carouse,
And is, to *Marks-men*, you'll allow,
For each his *Arrow*, and his *Bow*,
Much fitter to determine Lots;
The Center shewing nearest Shots:
The Day then, Sir, to celebrate,
And crown each *Archer's* lucky Fate,
The Muse your Company bespeaks,
To shoot, at least, for Ale and Cakes;
And, Sir, whoever wins the Prize,
To do him Justice to the Skies.

'Robin Hood's Answer'

Untouch'd by *Phoebus'* scorching Rays,
And his poetick Fire,
Victorious Laurel, not the Bays,
Is all my Soul's Desire.

Soon will the rash *Apollo* know,
The Danger of inviting,
An *Archer* armed with his Bow,
And Impliments for fighting.

The *Round* of Beef with all it's [*sic*] Charms,
Will small Protection yield,
Against an *Archer's* conquering Arms,
Tho' turn'd into a shield.

His *Butt* he'll make it, which shall feel,
The Marks of his Disdain,
His Arrows tipt with Blades of Steel,
Shall pierce thro' ev'ry Vein.

The Vict'ry gain'd, he scorns to boast,
For gen'rous Deeds renown'd;
Then to the *Round around* we'll toast
'Till all the World turns round.

Thus writeth in a merry mood,
Your humble Servant *Robin Hood.*

As Addison's remarks above illustrate, while English artists and writers in the eighteenth century looked to classical, continental culture for inspiration, they often desired to point out that the bravery of heroes from English history could rival any of those from Ancient Greece and Rome. Winstanley is continuing this idea: Robin Hood will indeed attend the feast of the archers, but he will beat any opponent who comes up against him. This will all be in good faith, of course, for after the archery contest all archers present will enjoy the feast.

Although a relatively minor figure in the eighteenth-century literary canon, Winstanley's work was subscribed to by a number of worthies including the Prince of Wales, Alexander Pope, and Jonathan Swift, the author of *Gulliver's Travels* (1726), who encouraged Winstanley to publish his collection. In total, there are nearly 200 subscribers listed in the front matter of Winstanley's book. For publishers, allowing wealthy patrons to subscribe and pay in advance for literary works meant that they could take commercial risks in publishing some books because they were assured that some of their costs would be met. The production of books was in fact an expensive process at this time, and many people, including the bourgeoisie, usually rented books from one of the many subscription libraries that were in operation at this time.

Along with reprints of early modern ballads in garlands, and poetry in the miscellanies, plays of Robin Hood were still popular. As we have seen, the May Games plays were no longer staged in provincial towns, but people still enjoyed their festivals. Successors to the Robin Hood May Day games were the Robin Hood plays that were staged at the Saint Bartholomew Fair in London, which were a regular feature at the fair's theatrical booths in the eighteenth and nineteenth centuries. It is at this fair that one of the earliest eighteenth-century Robin Hood plays entitled *Robin Hood and Little John* (1717) was first performed. Another play staged at the Bartholomew Fair was *Robin Hood: An Opera* (1730). This was not a high-end opera with finely composed music, however, for it was a ballad opera which incorporated the tunes of contemporary 'folk' ballads, although new lyrics were written for the play. This is just one of the airs in the play, all of which were quite short, that used a well-known tune with lyrics newly-written for the production:

Air V. *The Roger de Coverley*

Cease away, my Boys, this ill-tim'd noise,
Away, away.
A friendless Jar all Peace destroys;
Let's sport and play.
Be brisk and airy, dance and sing,,
And then away,
With Shouts to make the Wood-Lands ring,
And hunt our Prey.

The 'Roger de Coverley' is the name of an old country dance and tune, popular in rural areas (the name was also used by Addison as a fictional correspondent in his *Spectator* magazine, published between 1711 and 1714). Folk, or traditional ballad songs, were a good choice for the writer of *Robin Hood: An Opera* because, being a play that was acted on the makeshift 'theatrical booths' at the fair, it meant that no music was required. The players could have sung the tunes a capella, and many of them would have been recognised by the audience and players without requiring an orchestra. Other Georgian playwrights followed the practice of incorporating popular ballads into their operas, especially when they were telling stories of thieves. A notable example of this is John Gay's *The Beggar's Opera* (1728), which tells the story of the highwayman, Captain Macheath, who is a gallant and romantic figure. There is no suggestion, however, that Macheath is any kind of Robin Hood as he steals and generally keeps everything to himself. This is how many highwaymen were viewed in the Georgian period. They were not good outlaw figures as such, it was more the fact that they only allegedly took what they needed and were polite and civil about it.

We first meet Robin Hood, who is the Earl of Huntingdon in *Robin Hood: An Opera*, being placed under arrest on the king's orders. A scheming earl named Pembrook has decided that he wants to marry Matilda, who is Robin's fiancé and the king's sister (she is not called Marian in the play, so it differs from Munday in this respect). To accomplish his goals, Pembrook has managed to convince the king to declare Robin an outlaw. Robin decides to take to Sherwood Forest where he meets with Little John and the usual suspects. While an outlaw he displays his benevolence to all around by stealing from the rich and giving to the poor:

Enter a Poor Man, and his Wife, with a Child in her arms.

Outlaw. Stand –

Woman. Ah!

Outl. Deliver!

Wom. Ah Gentlemen! I have nothing to part with but my child; pray don't take that from me.

Man. Ah Gentlemen! I have nothing to part from but my wife, take her and welcome.

Robin H. The Fellow does not know what he says; – here, here, good People, there is something to relieve your Poverty. [*Gives a Bag.*]

P. M. Why, Captain, there is an Hundred Pounds.

Rob. H. So much the better, it will do 'em more good; it is my own Share I part with, Friend, I give nothing away.

P. M. Now I think Two-pence or Three-pence between 'em had been mighty handsome.

Man & Wom. Oh bless your Goodness, noble Master!

Rob. H. Let us ascend the Hill and seek our farther. Fortune with open Hands shall ever bless the Man who helps the Poor with his Success.

The 'Stand and Deliver' lines, which were famously said to have been uttered by many Georgian highwaymen – the era when this play was written being the golden age of highway robbery – de-historicise Robin Hood. It is in fact unclear whether this is a play that is set during the medieval period at all, for the king is left unnamed. It was also supposed to be a comical play, evident in instances such as the above when the farmer tells the outlaw that they are welcome to his wife and child. This would likely have elicited some knowing humour from players and audience members alike. Eventually, Robin comes face-to-face with Pembrook and the pair begin sparring. Robin mortally wounds him just as the king enters. With a dying speech Pembrook confesses that Robin never wronged him and that he has been justly punished. Robin Hood is therefore forgiven and the king permits him to marry Matilda.

The Bartholomew Fair was held in London on 24 August every year from 1133 until 1855. The founder of the Fair, a monk named Rahere, originally envisioned it as a fundraising event during which time people could enjoy themselves and also donate to local good causes. For a small fee merchants could come from far and wide and set up a stall there and sell their wares. There is no evidence to suggest that the behaviour of the patrons in the medieval fairs was anything but respectable. However, the behaviour of the clientele at this event became worse throughout the early modern period. By the time that *Robin Hood: An Opera* was staged, the Bartholomew Fair was an event at which drunkenness and debauchery reigned supreme. It was tolerated by Georgians for the most part, however, as members of the aristocracy enjoyed rude and rowdy entertainment just as much as their plebeian counterparts. It would have been a noisy event, not only because of the vast quantities of cheap alcohol available but also because there were exhibitions of wild animals from all over the world, fire-eaters, wrestling matches, and boxing competitions. In view of this, it is likely that the script served as a guide to what performers might say, but at the same time would have allowed for some interaction with the audience. In the next century, the fair was too much for Victorian moralists and, after a campaign highlighting its immorality, the event was abolished with the last fair taking place in 1855.

One character who appeared in *Robin Hood: An Opera* was George-a-Green, the pindar, or 'pound keeper of Wakefield'. Pound keepers in the medieval and early modern period were individuals that were hired by the state to round up stray animals and return them to their relevant owners. The office also existed in Colonial America and Australia in the eighteenth and nineteenth centuries. It was quite an important job in rural places whose local economy was primarily agricultural because stray animals would often destroy farmers' crops. The encounter between Robin Hood and the pindar in the play follows that which is found in early modern ballads, another one of those Robin-Hood-meets-his-match scenarios in which they fight and then the pindar joins Robin's band. This is how Robin's meeting with Pindar is related in the play:

> *Rob.* Who's he that dares to stop me in my Way?
>
> *Pin.* Who am I that dares to hop and dance? Why I am the Jolly Pindar of Wakefield – and tho' I'm a little grey in my Head, and dunny in my Ears, I have a Heart as sound as an Elm, and I don't fear the best Lad of you all.
>
> *Rob.* What means the sawcy Fool?
>
> *Pin.* Sawce for Fowl – by'r Lady, and Sawce for Fish too – Will you take a Stroke with me …
>
> [*Pindar and Robin Hood fight. Pindar strikes the Staff out of his Hand.*]
>
> *Pin.* Nea, take up they Staff again. I scorn to shew foul Play.
>
> *Rob.* Heartily hast thou fought – give me thy Hand and from this moment, Robin Hood's thy Friend.
>
> *Pin.* With all my Heart – here our divisions end.

This pound keeper probably had his own separate tradition originally, before his story became fused with Robin Hood. Sometimes it makes sense to view these early local figures as the equivalent of superheroes today: each superhero such as Captain America, Iron Man, or Wonder Woman has his or her own set of stories, realised by different authors, given different backstories, and at times representing a different ideology. As they do in movies such as *Avengers Assemble* (2012) and *Justice League* (2017), however, many of them meet up. *A Ballad of George and a Green* was published in 1557, although what remains of it now is degraded and exists only as a fragment, and it is unknown whether it originally included Robin Hood. A play, perhaps written by Robert Greene, the author of some of the rogue pamphlets referred to above, was performed in 1593 and published in 1599 under the title of *A Pleasant Conceyted Comedie of George a Greene, the Pinner of Wakefield*, which does include Robin Hood. The disagreement between Robin and George in Greene's play comes from Marian's instigation. She says that she is upset that whenever she ventures out of the forest, all she ever hears are songs celebrating the life of George-a-Green, while she never hears any of Robin Hood. The outlaws then decide to seek out George and prove to Marian that they are the manliest men in town:

Enter Robin Hood, Mayd Marian, Scarlet, and Much the Millers Sonne.

Robin. Why is not louely Marian blithe of cheere?
What ayles my Lemman that she gins to lower?
Say good Marian why art thou so sad?
Marian. Nothing my Robin grieues me to the heart,
But whensoeuer I doe walke abroad,
I heare no songs but all of George a Greene …

Robin. Content thee Marian, I will ease thy griefe,
My merrie men and I will thither stray,
And here I vow that for the loue of thee,
I will beate George a Green, or he shall beate me.

Obviously Munday cannot claim all of the credit for joining Robin and Marian, as the author of the *Conceyted Comedie* did it before him. Robin Hood then predictably loses the fight with George and afterwards, as in all Robin-Hood-meets-his-match scenarios, the pair join forces.

Another ballad appeared in the seventeenth century entitled *Robin Hood and the Jolly Pindar of Wakefield* (sometimes it is listed under a slightly varying title). The story is much the same, ending with the following:

O wilt thou forsake the pinder's craft,
And go to the green wood with me?
Thou shalt have a livery twice in the year,
The one green, the other brown.

If Michaelmas day were once come and gone
And my master had paid me my fee,
Then would I set as little by him
As my master doth set by me.
I'll take my bent bowe in my hand,
And come into the greenwood to thee.

An early English prose romance entitled *The Pinder of Wakefield: Being the Merry History of George a Greene*, was published in 1632, and again in 1706, which rehearses the themes of the ballad. Amateur historians from Wakefield have often used the story of Robin Hood's meeting with the pindar, along with Hunter's identification of a historical person named

Robert Hood who lived in Wakefield during the medieval period as evidence that the real Robin Hood was from that town. Journalists for local Wakefield-based newspapers, whenever they need a quick story, similarly draw upon this to no doubt stir up a bit of civic patriotism over the fact that a 'historical' hero came from the area. Yet for the same reason that we cannot class the *Gest* as a source of factual information on the life of any real Robin Hood, we cannot similarly assume that the story of George-a-Green contains anything factual either. As we have seen, *The Jolly Pinder of Wakefield* simply rehearses scenes that had been seen in many Robin Hood stories.

To return to the eighteenth century: some playwrights often took the plot of a single Robin Hood ballad and turned it into a play, as Moses Mendez did in *Robin Hood: A New Musical Entertainment* (1751), with accompanying music performed by the Society of the Temple of Apollo, founded by James Oswald (1711–69), who was Chamber Composer to George III. The individual song writers are not credited, as was usual practice at this time, but the following opening song remained popular into the nineteenth century when it appeared in cheap versions of *Robin Hood's Garland*, and J. M. Gutch's *A Lytell Geste of Robin Hode* (1847):

> As blithe as the Linnet sings in the green Wood,
> So blithe we'll wake the Morn;
> And thro' the wide Forest of merry *Sherwood*
> We'll wind the Bugle Horn.
>
> The Sheriff attempts to take bold *Robin Hood,*
> Bold *Robin* disdains to fly:
> Come on when he will, in merry *Sherwood*
> We'll vanquish, Boys, or die.
>
> Our Arrows shall drink of the fallow Deer's Blood,
> We'll hunt them all over the Plain;
> And thro' the fair Forest of merry *Sherwood,*
> No Shaft shall fly in vain.
>
> Brave *Scarlet* and *John,* who were never subdu'd,
> Give each his Hand so bold;
> We'll reign through the Forest of merry *Sherwood:*
> What say my Hearts of Gold?

Although this opening song promises an exciting fight between the Sheriff and the outlaws, it contains nothing of the sort and the story itself is an adaptation of a late sixteenth-century ballad entitled *Robin Hood and Allen-a-Dale*. The plot sees Robin meeting a poor lovesick man wandering in the forest, heartbroken because his lover is due to be married at her father's behest to another man who is richer than him; hence one of Robin's airs:

> I'll sing you a song that will suit us all round;
> The tale may displease, yet the moral is sound:
> A virgin as sweet as the morning in May,
> Once lov'd a young shepherd (of merit) they say.
> But her father refus'd him, for he had not gold,
> As av'rice too often will cleave to the old;
> To a coxcomb he'd giver, well furnished with pence,
> Who had ev'ry endowment-save honour and sense.

By the end of the play, due to Robin Hood's intervention, the two lovers are eventually married in Sherwood Forest. It was important in the eighteenth century that artistic and literary works had to be 'improving' or portray a moral in some way or other, which accounts for the stress on the fact that 'the moral is sound'. In this way such a work would sit well with polite audiences. The moral of the story, of course, is rather vague, being a general injunction to avoid avarice. The message one gets overall is that one should not stand in the way of true love, and that love should trump financial considerations.

Mendez's play was performed at the Theatre Royal, Drury Lane, which is an altogether more upmarket venue than a hastily crafted booth at Bartholomew Fair. Theatres Royal, or Patent Theatres, were establishments that had been granted a monopoly on serious spoken drama by the king after the Restoration. Other theatres which did not have a letter from the monarch authorising them to do so were only permitted to play comedies, pantomimes, and melodramas. The first of these Patent Theatres were the ones in Drury Lane and Lincolns-Inn-Fields. The appearance of a Robin Hood play at such an august establishment, along with the outlaw's appearances in the works of Dryden and Winstanley, indicate that Robin Hood in the eighteenth century was not just a figure encountered in low and vulgar ballads and plays, such as those performed at Bartholomew Fair, but was also a figure who was easily incorporated into high culture as well.

In the latter part of the eighteenth-century another Robin Hood play was staged at one of the Patent Theatres, although it pursues a more nationalist theme. This was Leonard MacNally's *Robin Hood; or, Sherwood Forest* (1784). When MacNally's play was being performed, Britain had just lost the American Revolutionary War (1776–83). Yet there was no bitterness from the British public towards George III. The prevailing opinion among many at home was that the American colonists had acted unreasonably. The public's frustrations at the loss of the American colonies and dent to national pride centred on the Prime Minister, Lord North, who resigned in 1782, while criticism of the king was muted. At any rate, the American Revolution sparked a new kind of nationalism in England, which was based upon loyalty to the monarch, the importance of the growing empire, and the value of a strong military and navy. Hints of this patriotism can be seen in MacNally's play; in the finale, for example, Robin, and his wife, Clorinda, sing:

> Strains of liberty we'll sing,
> To our country, queen, and king!
> To those friends who often here,
> With their smiles our bosoms cheer.

Similarly, when Thomas Evans compiled his collection of *Old Ballads, Historical and Narrative* (1777), which reprinted a number of Robin Hood songs, he was explicitly nationalist in his preface. The study of the popular culture of England's medieval past would, according to Evans, highlight everything that was good about the nation's history:

> Many of the ancient ballads have been transmitted to the present times; and in them the character of the nation displays itself in striking colours. The boastful history of her victories, the prowess of her favourite kings and captains, the wonderful adventures of the legendary saint and knight-errant, are the topics of rough rhyme and unadorned narration.

Apart from some of the ballads, however, most of the plays from the Georgian era (especially the plays) were quite forgettable – even if they did admittedly enjoy a good season or two in the theatre. While we do see a heroic Robin Hood in MacNally's play and some ballads, it was not until the very end of the century that Robin was truly transformed from the buffoonish ballad hero and the passive, melancholy dispossessed aristocrat, into a thief and freedom fighter – the image of our hero which most people have today.

Chapter 5

Revolution and Romanticism

How happy live we in the wood.
Beneath the sway of Robin Hood.
The deer with spreading antlers crowned
Stalks stately o'er the bower.

Robert Southey, *Harold; or,*
The Castle of Morford (1791)

With respect to his personal character: it is sufficiently evident
that he was active, brave, prudent, patient; possessed of
uncommon bodyly [*sic*] strength, and considerable military
skill; just, generous, benevolent, faithful, and beloved or
revered by his followers or adherents for his excellent and
amiable qualities.

Joseph Ritson, *Robin Hood* (1795)

I am a bad hand at depicting a hero properly so called, and
have an unfortunate propensity for the dubious characters of
borderers, highland robbers, and all others of a Robin Hood
description.

Walter Scott, July 1814

The history of the late eighteenth century Atlantic world was marked, as
Eric Hobsbawm argues, by two major revolutions: the industrial revolution
(c. 1760–c. 1820), and the French Revolution and the Napoleonic Wars
(1789–1815). The latter event is more relevant for our purposes. In Britain,
during the early years of the French Revolution, there was a great deal of

admiration for the French people who, many people believed, had finally thrown off the weight of absolutist government and were heading towards a form of constitutional government. The attitude of some people in Britain soured towards the revolution as they witnessed it descend into violence, especially once the Jacobins came to power in France and executed the French royal family. After their execution, the Reign of Terror commenced: the government of France, under the stewardship of the Committee of Public safety led by Robespierre, decided that mass executions were needed in order to safeguard the revolution from those who would seek to oppose it and do away with the people's new-found freedoms. They also had a new humane method of execution in the form of guillotine, which, so it was thought at the time, instantly killed the offender instead of strangling them for about fifteen minutes while dangling on the end of a rope. While many in England were perturbed by the bloodbath that was the Reign of Terror, some in England held steadfastly to the view that a revolution was also needed there. Thus, many English Jacobin clubs appeared throughout the country, with some of them even plotting the assassination of key members of the government.

One young radical was the poet, Robert Southey (1774–1843), who wrote the first Robin Hood novel. The future Poet Laureate was born in Bristol and, under the guardianship of his aunt, received a good education at various independent schools. He was a pioneering medievalist, authoring a number of narrative poems set during the Middle Ages, such as *Joan of Arc* (1796), and *Wat Tyler*, which was written in 1794 and published later in 1817. He also edited versions of the Norse saga *The Edda* (1807), as well as an edition of Thomas Malory's *Le Morte D'Arthur* in 1817. In addition, Southey introduced the first vampire into English literature in his poem entitled *Thalaba the Destroyer* (1801). He is also the author who first recorded in writing the folk tale of Goldilocks and the Three Bears in *The Doctor* (1837). His talents were not restricted merely retelling medieval stories and elaborating upon folk tales, however, for he could also speak Spanish and Portuguese fluently, and wrote a three volume *History of Brazil* between 1810 and 1819. His Robin Hood story, *Harold, or, The Castle of Morford* (1791), while as yet unpublished, is the first attempt by a writer, as far as can be ascertained, to adapt the Robin Hood story into that most famous of literary genres, the eighteenth-century novel, and it reveals some of the sources that this young man was reading at the time that he wrote it.

Southey is clearly evoking the gothic in his novel, and its opening sentence, 'it was night', anticipates the melodramatic 'dark and stormy night' opening to Edward Bulwer Lytton's highwayman novel *Paul Clifford* (1830). In *Harold*, we also read further tropes that are common to many gothic novels such as hidden family secrets, eerie prophecies, seemingly supernatural occurrences, and villainous aristocrats. The novel concerns the eponymous Harold who has been abroad for some years in the Holy Land and has recently returned to England. Wandering through Sherwood Forest, he muses upon the prospect of seeing his father after so long. As luck would have it, Harold then comes across his younger brother, Tancred, who is living as an outlaw because he has been falsely accused of murdering their father. Harold naturally breaks down in tears because of this, and eventually he and Robin Hood's paths cross and, along with Richard the Lionheart who has returned to England in disguise, resolves to seek revenge on the man who really killed his father, the murderous Baron Fitzosborne.

Southey is clearly acquainted with a wide range of Robin Hood literature. He likely read Ben Jonson's *The Sad Shepherd* (1641), for a couple of the characters in Southey's text bear the same names as those in Jonson's play. There is a humorous scene in which, having caught the Bishop of Hereford, when, having bound the prelate to a tree, the outlaws hold a mock trial for themselves which mimics the dramatic language of *The Newgate Calendar*:

> 'I confess for my part,' said Little John, 'having once met with the right reverend father, before whom we now stand, and feloniously, traitorously, and with evil intent having despoiled him of all the wealth he had with him and likewise afterwards tying him on a horse the wrong way, for which crimes most reverend prelate I humbly beg absolution.'

The inclusion of this mock trial suggests that Southey was acquainted with the stories of Robin Hood featured in works such as Smith's and Johnson's histories of highwaymen.

Throughout the eighteenth century, there was a lot of public interest in the lives of criminals. As a result, books telling their life stories were immensely popular throughout the eighteenth century. To illustrate just how popular criminal biographies were, it should be noted that after the Bible and Bunyan's *Pilgrims' Progress*, *The Newgate Calendar* was the third most common book to be found in the middle-class home. As well as Smith and Johnson's books, other notable examples include *The History of the Remarkable Life of John Sheppard* (1724), the life story of a boy thief who escaped from gaol four times. Another one, perhaps written by Daniel Defoe, is *An Authentick Narrative of the Life and Actions of Jonathan Wild* (1725), which is a biography of the eponymous 'Thief Taker General of Britain and Ireland', who led a double life as London's chief agent of law enforcement while simultaneously running an organised crime network. There were also serialised publications such as *The Proceedings of the Old Bailey* and *The Ordinary of Newgate's Account*. Even major eighteenth-century novelists capitalised upon the public interest in crime: Defoe drew inspiration from criminal biography in several novels including *Captain Singleton* (1720), *Moll Flanders* (1722), and *Colonel Jack* (1722). Henry Fielding authored *Jonathan Wild* (1743) which appropriated the life of the thief taker to critique the regime of the Prime Minister, Robert Walpole. While some of these works were expensive, there was something to suit poorer readers in the form of 'Last Dying Speeches', printed on broadsides, which, as their name suggests, allegedly recounted the last words of criminals before they stepped on to the gallows. The language used in such histories of the highwaymen were heavily moralistic, often serving as moralist texts: readers were meant to read about a criminal's way of life and avoid making the same mistakes that had led them to the gallows. Robin Hood receives a bad reputation in Smith's work, and is demoted from his recently acquired peerage in the sixteenth century to be portrayed as an unsavoury character. This is what Smith, in a passage that Johnson plagiarises almost word-for-word, says about Robin Hood:

> This bold robber, Robin Hood, was, some write, descended of the noble family of the earls of Huntingdon; but that is only fiction, for his birth was but very obscure, his pedigree *ab origine* being no higher than poor shepherds, who for some time lived in Nottinghamshire, in which county, at a little village adjacent to the Forest of Sherwood, he was born in the reign of King Henry the Second. He was bred up a butcher, but being of a very licentious, wicked inclination, he followed not his trade, but in the reign of King Henry the Second, associating himself with several robbers and outlaws, was chosen as their captain.

To return to Southey's novel: the fact that the Bishop of Hereford features in this story suggests that Southey is also acquainted with the broadsides and garlands that were being published in his lifetime, as the ballad of *Robin Hood and the Bishop of Hereford* was included in those publications.

Yet Southey's juvenile novel does not merely hark back to earlier Robin Hood texts but also anticipates future sources such as Walter Scott's *Ivanhoe* (1819). In *Harold*, just as King Richard does in Scott's novel, he returns to England in disguise and falls in with Robin Hood's gang of outlaws. The situation of Harold himself is similar in some respects to that of Ivanhoe's: he returns from the crusades to find a changed country, and eventually joins Robin Hood's gang along with King Richard. Scott's novel is also noteworthy for depicting the political situation in twelfth-century England as being one of a state of near civil war between the Anglo-Saxons and the Normans. Southey is the first to place Saxon names in a Robin Hood story. The names of some of Scott's characters include Athelstan and Elfrida, and in *Harold* we see Athelstan (often incorrectly spelled as Athelwold throughout Southey's novel) and Ulfrida. While no documentary evidence exists to say that Scott, who was friends with Southey, ever saw *Harold*, perhaps the two men did at least exchange ideas on the subject a couple of decades later when Scott was writing *Ivanhoe*, for the similarities between the two novels appear to be more than just circumstantial.

In his youth, Southey enthusiastically supported the French Revolution that was occurring across the channel, as did many contemporary Romantic poets such as William Wordsworth (1770–1850) and Samuel Taylor Coleridge (1772–1834). 'Bliss it was in that dawn to be alive', Wordsworth would exclaim in *The Prelude* (1799). In order to express similar sympathies with the revolution occurring in France, Southey, in many of his works, looked back to the medieval period. In one of his later works, *Wat Tyler* (1794), the hero of the Peasants' Revolt (1381) is depicted as a hard-working labouring man who fights to end the tyranny of Richard II's reign. In *Harold*, Richard I is an enlightened king who wishes to reform the political landscape and improve the lot of poor people in his kingdom. Upon becoming lost in the forest after having returned from his crusading adventures he is impressed at the egalitarian constitution of the outlaws' society, exclaiming, 'For God … were there such a band of outlaws in every forest in England we should not have many poor!'

While Southey may have been a radical in his youth and wished for a similar revolution to engulf Britain, as a result of the Reign of Terror in France, his heart slowly hardened against the cause of political reforms and he gradually abandoned radical politics, becoming increasingly conservative in his political outlook. Eventually, in 1813, he was appointed Poet Laureate, a position which requires its incumbent to 'write to order', and to shower the monarchy and the political establishment with praise. Southey would go on to write another Robin Hood work later in his life. This was a poem which was published posthumously as *Robin Hood: A Fragment* (1847). It is a minor work and was quickly forgotten about by the public, and very few academics study it. However, in the 1790s, shortly after Southey wrote *Harold*, there was another man researching the Robin Hood legend who did not forsake his revolutionary ideology, even in the face of the carnage across the channel, and he is one of the most interesting characters in eighteenth-century literary history, Joseph Ritson (1752–1803).

Ritson's *Robin Hood* was published in 1795. He was a northerner, born in Stockton-on-Tees, and entered the legal profession at an early age. His real passion lay not in the dry conveyancing work he was undertaking, but in the study of Old and Middle English texts. In his spare time he visited libraries and archives to study a variety of manuscript sources. He carefully transcribed these documents and made them available to the reading public in a variety of volumes such as *Select Collection of English Songs* (1783), *Pieces of Ancient Popular Poetry* (1791), and *The Northumberland Garland* (1793). It was Ritson who 'rediscovered' medieval Robin Hood texts such as *A Gest of Robyn Hode* (c. 1450), which had been virtually forgotten by the late eighteenth century, and reprinted them in an accessible form. He also included in his collection every other early modern Robin Hood ballad that he could find, although he did not know about the existence of *Robin Hood and the Monk*. His tireless quest to bring new sources to light and advance people's understanding of English history meant that, along with Thomas Percy, the editor of the *Reliques*, he was soon looked upon as an authority on the subject by many contemporary authors. For example, in Walter Scott's *The Antiquary* (1816), the eponymous antiquary, Jonathan Oldbuck, upon hearing a woman singing an old song gets very excited at having discovered an old ballad and exclaims that 'Ritson could not impugn its authenticity!' Ritson's authority on Robin Hood, and indeed upon many other traditional folk songs, was only surpassed in the late nineteenth century when Francis J. Child was collating folk songs for publication in a multivolume series of books entitled *The English and Scottish Popular Ballads* (1882–98).

Yet Ritson did not merely transcribe and publish the archival material that he found, he also wrote critical essays on them and other literary subjects. He could be fierce towards his rival antiquaries, evident by the numerous times he attacked the allegedly shoddy work of Thomas Percy and John Pinkerton in the press. Southey recognised Ritson's contribution to historical scholarship in spite of his irascible temper, however, and later remarked that 'Joseph Ritson is the oddest, but most honest of all our antiquarians, and he abuses Percy and Pinkerton with less mercy than justice'. The idea that Ritson was the most honest of all contemporary historians had some merit: Percy and Pinkerton often edited violent or vulgar parts out of the ballads which they published in order not to offend the polite sensibilities of their predominantly bourgeois readers. In Percy's edit of *Robin Hood and Guy of Gisborne*, when Little John shoots the Sheriff of Nottingham through the chest, as happens in the original ballad, Percy changed this and had John shoot the sheriff in the backside. It is a strange edit and the reasons why he did it remain unclear because although he probably did this to avoid offending polite readers, he left in the part where Robin cuts of Guy's head and mangles his face.

Nevertheless, Ritson was not perfect and certainly had his own critics. Although he portrayed himself, usually with good reason, as the most honest antiquary at the time, he often accepted source material uncritically and held that entirely fictional sources were factual. He took it as a given that Robin Hood was an earl, for example, and in support of his argument drew upon Munday's plays, the chronicles that ascribe 'nobility' to Robin, as well as a contrived family tree written by a contemporary, Dr William Stukeley. This family tree showed that Robin Hood was allegedly descended from Walthoef, the Earl of Northumbria (d. 1076) and his wife, Judith, the Countess of Huntingdon. Stukeley, the author of this ingenious fabrication, probably wanted to imply from this family tree that he was related in some way to the Will Stutely, or Stutly, of some early modern Robin Hood ballads.

Most of the criticisms of Ritson by commentators in the press, however, were directed, not so much towards his work as towards his politics. As we have seen, Ritson was an outspoken republican and, like young Southey, was an enthusiastic supporter of the French Revolution and the ideals enshrined in The Declaration of the Rights of Man and Citizen. Whereas Southey and other Romantics abandoned their radical principles after the beginning of the Reign of Terror, it did not bother Ritson: he remained steadfast in his beliefs until his death. Upon a visit to Paris at the height of the Revolution, he wrote a letter to his friend, whom he addressed as 'Citizen', in accordance with revolutionary ideas, that,

> I admire the French more than ever. They deserved to be free
> and they really are so. You have read their new constitution:
> can anything be more admirable? We, who pretend to be free,
> you know, have no constitution at all.

Holding steadfastly to revolutionary beliefs, after the commencement of the Reign of Terror and then the Revolutionary and Napoleonic Wars was a brave and bold thing for Ritson to do: in 1794, the year before Ritson published *Robin Hood*, the Prime Minister, William Pitt (1759–1806), initiated a series of repressive measures aimed at stifling the growth of revolutionary sentiment in Britain. Habeas corpus was suspended and many advocates for reform found themselves under surveillance by the authorities and some had even been arrested. According to his letters, it is evident that Ritson believed that he too was being watched by the police.

Having felt unable to express his own radical politics for fear of government repression, he infused revolutionary sentiments into his biography of Robin Hood, which is prefaced to his ballad collection. Ritson's Robin Hood appears almost as a medieval Thomas Paine (a prominent revolutionary thinker during both the American and French Revolutions). Ritson argues that Robin Hood was no mere thief but a freedom fighter:

> In these forests, and with this company, he for many years reigned like an independent sovereign; at perpetual war, indeed, with the King of England, and all his subjects, with an exception, however, of the poor and needy, and such as were 'desolate and oppressed,' or stood in need of his protection.

Ritson further elaborates upon Robin Hood's virtuous qualities, calling him active, brave, wise, and of almost superhuman strength:

> A man who, in a barbarous age and under a complicated tyranny, displayed a spirit of freedom and *independence*, which has endeared him to the common people, whose cause he maintained, (for all opposition to tyranny is the cause of the people) and, in spite of the malicious endeavours of pitiful monks, by whom history was consecrated to the crimes and follies of sainted idiots and titled ruffians, to suppress all record of his patriotic exertions and patriotic acts, will render his name immortal.

While some literary magazine reviewers saw straight through Ritson's attempts to impose his own politics on to a historical subject, to the average reader, this likely appeared as the authoritative and definitive final word on the subject of Robin Hood.

Ritson died in 1803, having had frequent bouts of mental illness throughout his life. In September of that year, he barricaded himself in his room and violently tried to attack all who approached him. After medical professionals managed to get him sedated, he was removed to the country house of Sir Jonathan Miles and attended to by doctors. Sadly, he died four days later. Eric Hobsbawm says that 'one might say that the intellectuals had ensured the survival of the bandits'. That statement rings true in the case of Ritson: he made medieval Robin Hood texts accessible and was the first historian to provide a biography for Robin Hood that was seemingly founded upon facts. His book would go on to influence portrayals of Robin Hood in the works of Walter Scott and Thomas Love Peacock.

Shortly after Ritson, an entirely new Robin Hood ballad entitled *The Birth of Robin Hood* appeared in an unlikely place: Scotland, recorded by a woman named Anna Gordon. She was born in Aberdeen in 1747 and was the daughter of Thomas Gordon, a Professor of Humanities, and Lilias Forbes. She grew up in a Scotland where ballads and folk songs were central to both elite and popular culture. The most significant ballad transcribed, from Mrs Brown follows the daughter of Earl Richard who falls in love with a servant named Willie. The daughter knows that her father will disapprove of such a union and so she and Willie resort to secretive meetings in the forest. Not unexpectedly she soon becomes pregnant and when she is about to give birth she absconds from her home and takes to the woods. Realising that his daughter is missing, the earl convenes a search party and goes out after her. He finds his daughter in the wood, exhausted from having given birth. Despite the circumstances of the illegitimate birth the earl is overcome with happiness upon seeing the child:

> He kist him o'er and o'er again:
> 'My grandson I thee claim;
> And Robin Hood in the gude green wood,
> And that shall be your name.'

It is unlikely that this ballad was ever popular like the old early modern songs of Robin Hood were but it was included in subsequent scholarly publications such as John Mathew Gutch's Robin Hood ballad anthology. However, the scholarly consensus regarding the authenticity of this ballad's place within the Robin Hood canon was soon challenged, most likely because it was neither medieval nor early modern in origin, but in all likelihood was Gordon's own creation. In the late nineteenth century, F. J. Child renamed the ballad *Willie and Earl Richard's Daughter* and did not place it alongside the other Robin Hood ballads in his *English and Scottish Popular Ballads*. Modern scholars have been similarly dismissive of Gordon's song. Dobson and Taylor remarked that 'Mrs Brown's ballad owes nothing but Robin Hood's name to the native English cycle of stories [...and] it remains suspicious that for the missing story of [Robin Hood's] birth we have to wait until the recitation of a remarkable Scottish woman delivered five years after the first (1795) edition of Ritson's comprehensive collection'. In spite of historians' objections to Anna Gordon's *Birth of Robin Hood*, it has become part of the overall corpus of Robin Hood stories as many late-Victorian children's authors use her ballad and retell it in prose.

A character that was loosely based upon Anna Gordon appears in the first published Robin Hood novel entitled *Robin Hood: A Tale of the Olden Time* (1819). The first half of the novel is devoted entirely to its framing narrative which is set during the eighteenth century, and sees a young man visiting an old professor who taught him at Oxford. Their conversation progresses to a discussion of early modern ballads, and the man's former tutor tells him that in the village where he lives there is a woman whose family has passed down songs of Robin Hood since time immemorial. So this pair and a few of their neighbours descend on the old woman's house to hear a tale of Robin Hood. The plot is simply a gothic inheritance drama with a flimsy medieval setting. It never went to a second edition and was only revived when Robin Hood scholar Stephen Knight edited and published the *Robin Hood Classic Fiction Library* in 2004. Besides, it was published in 1819, and readers had a much more enjoyable portrayal of Robin Hood in that year when Scott's *Ivanhoe* was published.

Percy, Southey, and Ritson were writing at the time of what was a European-wide cultural revolution: the era of Romanticism. It was an artistic and literary mode that eschewed the formalism and classicism that had prevailed in high culture since the seventeenth century, in part due to the excesses of the French Revolution, and instead aimed to reconnect with the natural world and national heritage. Of course, a writer such as Southey would not have called himself a Romantic, for the term was a later Victorian invention, but medievalism in the early nineteenth century became more popular than ever, especially under a new generation of Romantics led by Walter Scott, Thomas Love Peacock, and John Keats.

REVOLUTION AND ROMANTICISM

Before we discuss the works of Scott and Peacock, let us take a detour into the world of Romantic-era poetry. As Romantics aimed to return to nature, many of their poems were written with rural themes and settings. Yet this rural world idealised by the Romantics was, in some parts of Britain, disappearing before their eyes. In the early nineteenth century, Britain was in the midst of the industrial revolution which began in the mid- to late eighteenth century, and continued apace until around 1820. While debate exists about the extent to which the industrialisation really was a 'revolution' and not simply an 'evolution', it cannot be denied that substantial changes occurred during this era. In the year 1700, for example, it is estimated that thirteen per cent of the population in England lived in an urban area, while that figure had risen to twenty-four per cent by 1800. Gradually throughout this period working practices changed as industry moved out of homes into factories where working time and wages were dictated by the factory clock. Factories were becoming a regular sight throughout the country, so much so that Blake makes reference to 'dark satanic mills' in *Milton* (1804). As one of the aims of the Romantic movement was to reconnect with the natural world, the forest and mountain dwelling outlaws of the past became nostalgic figures for some poets. Wordsworth, for example, wrote the following lines about the Scottish highland chieftain, Rob Roy, and made an explicit connection to Robin Hood:

> A famous man is Robin Hood,
> The English ballad-singer's joy!
> And Scotland has a thief as good,
> An outlaw of as daring mood;
> She has her brave Rob Roy!
> Then clear the weeds from off his Grave,
> And let us chant a passing stave,
> honour of that Hero brave!

The same highlander was immortalised in 1817 by Sir Walter Scott in his novel *Rob Roy* (1817).

The pre-industrial world of medieval England is glorified by John Keats in his poem *Robin Hood: To a Friend*, written in 1818 but published later in Keats's anthology entitled *Lamia, Isabella, and the Eve of St Agnes* (1820). Keats's poem was originally sent to a friend of his, John Hamilton Reynolds, as part of a literary exchange between the two men upon the subject of Robin Hood. It was not unusual in the nineteenth century, or indeed in preceding centuries for that matter, for poets to exchange verses through letter writing. Reynolds commenced the literary exchange and in his poem, in accordance with the Romantics' desire to get back in touch with nature, Reynolds argues that the days of Robin Hood and the merry greenwood can be resurrected if one simply were to travel to Sherwood Forest and reconnect with Robin's old hunting grounds once again:

> The trees in Sherwood forest are old and good, –
> The grass beneath them now is dimly green;
> Are they deserted all? Is no young mien,
> With loose slung bugle, met within the wood?
> No arrow found, – foil'd of its antler food, –
> Struck in the oak's rude side? – Is there nought seen,
> To mark the revelries which there have been,
> In the sweet days of merry Robin Hood?
> Go there, with summer, and with evening – go,
> In the soft shadows like some wandering man,
> And thou shalt far amid the forest know
> The archer men in green, with belt and bow,
> Feasting on pheasant, river fowl, and swan,
> With Robin at their head, and Marian.

Keats has a more pessimistic view, however, and he disagrees with Reynolds because he can see that industrial capitalism has forever harmed the natural world and it is impossible to recapture even the spirit of times gone by:

> No! those days are gone away,
> And their hours are old and gray,
> And their minutes buried all,
> Under the downtrodden pall.
> Of the leaves of many years.

There are two meanings of the word 'pall', and either of these would fit into Keats's lamentation of the loss of the medieval period. In the first instance, it means a type of funeral cloth which is placed over a coffin, which of course would merge into Keats's vision of the irrecoverable loss, or death, of the idyllic 'merrie England'. Furthermore, we saw earlier that even in 1804, Blake criticised the fact that industrialisation was taking hold rapidly and spoiling the green and pleasant land that England once was. Another meaning of the word 'pall' is that of a dark cloud of smoke or dust. This is equally applicable given the fact this was the period in which smoke pollution became an environmental problem, as 'dark Satanic mills' spewed forth large quantities of thick black smoke from their towers. While complaints about pollution caused by coal smoke have been voiced since the medieval period, black smoke became a signifier of the modern industrial city. New towns and cities could often be buried under a 'pall' for days at a time. The use of coal in industry, as well as domestic consumption of coal, contributed to the sharp rise in coal burning in early nineteenth-century Britain, with 15 million tonnes being burned annually by the year 1800. Even at this early stage there were reactions to the effects of the pollution that the increasing burning of coal for fuel was having on the urban environment: in Manchester, for example, Thomas Percival (1740–1804) established a municipal board of health, and he and the board regarded the combatting of smoke pollution as one of the most important issues of the day. Smoke pollution affected not only people's health but the landscape as well. Buildings were gradually blackened and this in turn affected the way that people dressed: fashion became darker and even then clothing became soiled with soot as it was hung out to dry. Thriving businesses were set up as early as 1772 to refurbish clothes that had been smoked. While numerous cities in Britain were suffering from heavy smoke pollution by 1800, it was not until the mid- to late nineteenth centuries that many of the national and regional smoke abatement societies were founded, and the government finally took steps towards cleaning Britain's air only during the 1950s.

It was not simply with smoke pollution that Keats was concerned, however, but also with deforestation in nineteenth-century industrial Britain. Romantic poets can be counted as early conservationists. Their fondness for the beauties of the natural world made them sensitive to environmental changes within their communities. Keats, therefore, imagines what Robin Hood and Maid Marian's reactions would be if they were resurrected during the nineteenth century:

> And if Robin should be cast
> Sudden from his turfed grave [...]
> He would swear, for all his oaks,
> Fall'n beneath the dockyard strokes,
> Have rotted on the briny seas.

It is estimated that in the entire history of the European continent – from pre-historic times to the twentieth century – over 537,000 square kilometres of indigenous woodland has been cleared. The process of deforestation reached its height between 1750 and 1849, the period in which Keats was writing, when 186,000 square kilometres of woodland were cleared in Europe alone. Sherwood Forest itself has undergone extensive deforestation throughout its history; in medieval times the forest covered over 100,000 acres, yet in modern times the forest covers a mere 450 acres; the forest which Robin and Marian loved has practically vanished. The main factors contributing to deforestation during the early nineteenth century were wood extraction for commercial purposes and agricultural expansion. However, as Keats observes, ships and dockyards were also significant factors in deforestation due to Britain's imperial ambitions as this was still the age of sail and all of the British Empire's ships were constructed from wood. As Mosley notes, timber was a key strategic resource, much like oil today, and the British fought three wars in Burma in 1824–26, 1852, and 1885–86 to gain access to the region's plentiful teak forests.

However, the poem is not simply a lamentation over a changing landscape but is also a critique of capitalism. To Keats, the medieval period was idyllic because it was a time when 'men knew nor rent nor leases'. In the modern world, in contrast, everything had its price. When Keats resurrects Marian into the nineteenth century, we see her as weeping:

> And if Marian should have,
> Once again her forest days [...]
> She would weep, that her wild bees,
> Sang not to her – strange! That honey,
> Can't be got without hard money.

The sweet honey which Marian enjoyed free of charge while she was living in the medieval greenwood was now a consumer commodity which she would have to pay for were she to be resurrected in the nineteenth century. Later in the century, Karl Marx and Frederich Engels would write in *The Communist Manifesto* (1848) that modern industrial society had created a system which 'has left no other nexus between man and man than naked self-interest, than callous cash payment'. This is not to suggest, of course, that Keats was anything like a communist, just that he had an awareness of the social and economic problems occurring concomitantly with the rise, and often as a result of, industrial capitalism. The world of 'merrie England' is lost forever and all that remains is to honour the outlaws' memories:

So it is: let us sing,
Honour to the old bow-string!
Honour to the bugle-horn!
Honour to the woods unshorn!
Honour to the Lincoln green!
Honour to the archer keen!
Honour to tight Little John,
And the horse he rode upon!
Honour to Bold Robin Hood,
Sleeping in the underwood!
Honour to Maid Marian,
And to all the Sherwood clan!
Though their days have hurried by,
Let us two a burden try.

In 1819, one year after Keats wrote *Robin Hood: To a Friend*, the most influential Robin Hood novel of the nineteenth and twentieth centuries was published: *Ivanhoe*, by Walter Scott, who is perhaps the most famous Scottish novelist who ever lived. Born in Edinburgh in 1771, he was articled to the legal profession after completing his studies. Since the days of his youth, however, he devoted himself to antiquarian pursuits in his leisure time, avidly reading scholarly works such as Percy's *Reliques*:

I then first became acquainted with Bishop Percy's *Reliques of Ancient Poetry*. As I had been from infancy devoted to legendary lore of this nature, and only reluctantly withdrew my attention, from the scarcity of materials and the rudeness of those which I possessed, it may be imagined, but cannot be described, with what delight I saw pieces of the same kind which had amused my childhood, and still continued in secret the Delilahs of my imagination, considered as the subject of sober research, grave commentary, and apt illustration, by an editor who showed his poetical genius was capable of emulating the best qualities of what his pious labour preserved. I remember well the spot where I read these volumes for the first time. It was beneath a huge platanus-tree, in the ruins of what had been intended for an old-fashioned arbor in the garden I have mentioned. The summer day sped onward so fast that, notwithstanding the sharp appetite of thirteen, I forgot the hour of dinner, was sought for with anxiety, and was still found entranced in my intellectual banquet. To read and to remember was in this instance the same thing, and henceforth I overwhelmed my schoolfellows, and all who would hearken to me, with tragical recitations from the ballads of Bishop Percy. The first time, too, I could scrape a few shillings together, which were not common occurrences with me, I bought unto myself a copy of those beloved volumes; nor do I believe I ever read a book half so frequently, or with half the enthusiasm.

Inspired by Percy, whose three volume work was a collection of Old- and Middle-English poetry, Scott went on to publish *Minstrelsy of the Scottish Border* (1802–03), which was an anthology of old Scots songs. Scott did not merely produce scholarly editions of old texts, however, for he was also a poet, authoring several lengthy narrative poems, most of which were set during the Middle Ages or the early modern period: *The Lay of the Last Minstrel, Harold the Dauntless, Marmion, The Lady of the Lake, Rokeby*, and *Lord of the Isles*. His poetry nowadays is rarely read by the general public, and it is his novels for which he is chiefly remembered. He authored over twenty-five novels, most of which are now known as the *Waverley Novels*.

Most of his novels dealt with the fairly recent Scottish past, in particular the eighteenth century. *Waverley*, which was the first historical novel in Western fiction, dealt with the Jacobite Rebellion of 1745. His second novel *Guy Mannering* (1815) is a tale set in Scotland during the 1760s, while his third novel, the aforementioned *Antiquary*, is set in Scotland during the 1790s. With *Ivanhoe*, Scott made a departure from Scottish history by writing a novel set in England during the medieval period. There were a few problems in the production of the novel, such as a lack of quality paper, and at one point while he was writing it, Scott's health deteriorated. But in December 1819, just in time for Christmas, *Ivanhoe* was ready for retail, bound in three small octavo volumes and selling at a quite hefty price of thirty-one shillings (all first editions of *Ivanhoe*, however, carry the date of 1820 on their title page, as it was originally scheduled for a release in January of the New Year).

Scott saw himself as one of the gentlemen antiquaries of the eighteenth century, such as Percy or Ritson. Scott maintained a cordial correspondence with Ritson and seems to have been the only one who could handle Ritson's frequent mood changes due to his mental health problems. In spite of Ritson's eccentricities, Scott recognised his contribution to contemporary scholarship and wrote the following lines about him:

REVOLUTION AND ROMANTICISM

As bitter as gall, and as sharp as a razor,
And feeding on herbs as a Nebuchadnezzar,
His diet too acid, his temper too sour,
Little Ritson came out with his two volumes more.

(Ritson was, unusually for this period, a vegetarian, which explains why he is seen 'feeding on herbs' in Scott's little poem). Reflecting Scott's love of antiquarian pursuits, the preface to *Ivanhoe* purports to be a letter sent from one (fictional) antiquary, Laurence Templeton, to the (also fictional) Rev. Dr Dryasdust, a name which is clearly meant to evoke an image of a white-haired old historian who sits among books and manuscripts all day. The story of *Ivanhoe*, we are told, is taken from an ancient manuscript in the possession of Sir Arthur Wardour. Readers of Scott's novels would have realised that this was another fictional character, taken from *The Antiquary*. The purpose of the novel, Templeton writes, is to celebrate English national history in popular culture, especially when no one until that date had attempted to:

> I cannot but think it strange that no attempt has been made to excite an interest for the traditions and manners of Old England, similar to that which has been obtained in behalf of those of our poorer and less celebrated neighbours.

According to Scott, England is in need of national heroes to celebrate, just as Scotland had them through Scott's novels such as *Rob Roy*, Thus,

> The name of Robin Hood, if duly conjured with, should raise a spirit as soon as that of Rob Roy; and the patriots of England deserve no less their renown in our modern circles, than the Bruces and Wallaces of Caledonia.

There are two outlaws listed there, along with one rebel king and one freedom fighter. Scott loved tales of outlaws and rebels from an early age. When he was a boy, Scott became disabled as a result of contracting polio in early childhood. In order to try and cure his disability, he was sent by his parents from Edinburgh into the rural Sandy-Knowe to live with relatives in the hope that the country environment would be good for him (throughout his youth, he was often subjected to some very odd remedies to try and cure his 'lameness'). It is while living at Sandy-Knowe he learned tales of heroic outlaws from his grandmother, as he said in his autobiography: 'my grandmother used to tell me many a tale of Watt of Harden, Wight Willie of

Aikwood, Jamie Telfer of the Fair Dodhead, and other heroes – merry men all of the persuasion and calling of Robin Hood and Little John'. This love of a rogue which developed in his youth even survived into adulthood, not just in his writings but also in his often humane treatment towards petty thieves and poachers; one of his best friends throughout his life was Thomas 'Tam' Purdie (1767–1829), whom Scott (a magistrate by the early 1800s), first met when he appeared before him in the dock accused of poaching; instead of fining or committing to gaol, Scott took pity upon Purdie and gave him a job as a groundskeeper on his estate. Thus, an admiration for criminals, as well as the fact that he was a skilled historian, meant that Scott could create an extremely detailed and exciting vision of the medieval past.

Scott's novel is set during the 1190s, and England is in a parlous state. It is a society that is essentially one of two nations and divided along racial lines between the Normans and the Anglo-Saxons:

> A circumstance which tended greatly to enhance the tyranny of the nobility, and the sufferings of the inferior classes, arose from the consequences of the Conquest by William Duke of Normandy. Four generations had not sufficed to blend the hostile blood of the Normans and Anglo-Saxons, or to unite, by common language and mutual interests, two hostile races, one of which still felt the elation of triumph, while the other groaned under all the consequences of defeat.

Why Scott chose to depict Robin as specifically Anglo-Saxon is unclear; perhaps he did indeed converse with his friend Robert Southey about his earlier Robin Hood novel. Scott was definitely acquainted with Ritson's *Robin Hood*, and, being the diligent scholar that he was, probably pored over Ritson's footnotes which say that, by the eighteenth century, Lincoln green was often referred to as Saxon green. While Scott's depiction of divisions between Saxon and Norman were racialist, in keeping with contemporary ideas about the divisions between certain ethnic groups being a question of racial difference, he was not racist. He did not view any 'race' as superior to another, and it was only later in the Victorian period that concepts of Anglo-Saxon racial supremacy would emerge. The divisions between the Anglo-Saxons and the Normans come to a head while Richard I is captured by Leopold of Austria, and his brother John rules as Regent. John taxes the people heavily to pay King Richard's ransom. In reality, John is hoarding the money for himself, hoping to raise an army to overthrow the few remaining barons who support Richard, while buying the others off. Unbeknownst to John and his Templar henchmen, Richard has also returned to England in disguise. Finding his land in chaos as a result of his brother's misrule, Richard allies with the Anglo-Saxons and the outlaw known as Robin of Locksley so he can regain control of his kingdom and thereby unite the Saxons and the Normans into one nation. Added into this plot are vividly exciting scenes which include jousting matches, archery tournaments, damsels in distress, and epic sieges and battles.

Scott completely invented the idea that the Anglo-Saxons and the Normans were at odds with each other in the 1190s. He did this because he had a message for nineteenth-century readers: society does not have to be divided the way that it was in the 1190s. The seating at the Ashby Tournament at the beginning of *Ivanhoe*, so argues Paul J. de Gategno, illustrates how divided English society is. The Saxons and the Normans are separated, while the burghers, who represent commercial interests, clamour for more prominence. Yet throughout the novel, Scott argues that if all classes of society work together, they can overcome their differences and build a stronger, better nation. This is symbolised in the alliance between the yeoman Robin of Locksley (used by Scott to symbolise the working classes, even though the term 'yeoman' in its medieval context corresponded to someone of middling status), Ivanhoe (the middle class), and Richard (royalty/aristocracy). Each class has responsibilities towards, and should endeavour to serve, one another, which would result in harmony between the classes. Thus, medieval feudalism, where each class owed loyalty to the other, could, Scott argued, be adapted for the nineteenth century.

England in 1819 was beset with class conflict: the Napoleonic Wars brought in their wake a trade and financial depression along with mass unemployment. The working classes and the middle classes did not have the right to vote, and many of the 'new' towns such as Manchester and Leeds, which since the eighteenth century had grown in size and economic importance, were not represented in Parliament. Conversely, 'rotten boroughs' such as Old Sarum in Wiltshire, which was a just field containing a cottage by 1819, returned two MPs. The political establishment, composed of a narrow oligarchy of aristocrats and landowners, had also implemented the hated Corn Laws in 1815. These were tariffs placed on imports of grain which were designed to protect the interests of wealthy farmers and landowners by keeping the price of grain, and therefore the price of bread, high. This led to extreme hunger for many working-class families at a time when the only employment they could secure was casual and poorly paid. Two years before Scott was writing, in 1817, the authorities had to put down a riot at Spa Fields, London, which was led by a Dr Watson, who was nicknamed 'Wat Tyler' in the press. In order to frighten the largely aristocratic ruling class, Wat's mob had raised the French tricolour as they marched, thereby raising the spectre of revolution and, of course, of the Reign of Terror. Additionally, between 1811 and 1816, workers who were angry with the fact that increasing industrialisation was devaluing their work began to vandalise many of the new machines that industrialists were installing in their factories throughout the midlands and the north of England. Demand for reform was in the air. Issues came to a head in 1819, while Scott was working on *Ivanhoe*, in Manchester. Peaceful protesters had gathered in St Peter's Fields to hear the radical reformer, Henry Hunt, speak upon the issue of parliamentary reform. In a similar manner to Dr Watson, Hunt was also equated with Wat Tyler in both the radical and conservative press. However, the magistrate ordered the local militia, many of whom were drunk, to charge at the peaceful protesters. A bloodbath ensued. It is estimated that fifteen people died and over 700 were injured. Scott himself was horrified by this event, and the general state of the nation. This is why we see all classes of people working together in *Ivanhoe*. Far from being a Wat Tyler figure however, Robin Hood is the saviour of the nation in *Ivanhoe*, and the upper classes need the working classes as much as the working classes rely on their 'betters'. Modern Robin Hood scholars are sometimes reluctant to include *Ivanhoe* fully as part of the later Robin Hood tradition. When the *Robin Hood Classic Fiction Library* was published back in 2005, it was not included. But we owe our modern conceptualisation of Robin Hood almost entirely to Scott, and of course Ritson. Robin of Locksley in *Ivanhoe* is a freedom fighter first, and an outlaw second. This is the model followed in almost every modern portrayal of the Robin Hood story.

Reviews of *Ivanhoe* were generally positive and even before its official release, the number of pre-orders for the new novel by the 'Author of Waverley' were staggering: the publisher, Robert Caddell, wrote to his business partner, Archibald Constable, that 'the orders for *Ivanhoe* increase amazingly – they now come nearly to 5000'. One reviewer in *La Belle Assemblée* wrote that 'this still nameless author prepares us, in every story which falls from his matchless pen, for all that is interesting, and far beyond the usual style of other works of fiction.' Mary Russell Mitford wrote to her friend, Sir William Elford, in 1820, and asked the following:

> Have you read *Ivanhoe*? Do you like it? What a silly question! What two silly questions! You must have read, and you must

have liked that most gorgeous and magnificent tale of chivalry. I know nothing so rich, so splendid, so profuse, so like old painted glass or a gothic chapel full of shrines and banners and knightly monuments. The soul, too, which is sometimes wanting, is there in its full glory of passion and tenderness.

Another anecdote written by Lady Louisa Scott (1807–52), who was no relation to Walter Scott, must have brought a smile to Scott's face:

Every body in this house has been reading an odd new kind of book called *Ivanhoe*, and nobody, as far as I have observed, has willingly laid it down again till finished. By this I conclude its success will fully equal that of its predecessors, notwithstanding it has quite abandoned their ground and ploughed up a field hitherto untouched. The interest of it indeed is most powerful; few things in prose or verse seize upon one's mind so strongly, are read with such breathless eagerness as the storming of the castle related by Rebecca, and her trial at Templestowe, Few characters ever were so forcibly painted as hers; the Jew too, the Templar, the courtly knight De Bracey, the wavering inconstant wickedness of John, are all worthy of Shakespeare.

Scott published all of his novels anonymously, having assumed the pseudonym of the 'Author of Waverley'. Lady Scott would not have known that the man to whom she was writing was in fact the author of Waverley.

There were not many dissenting voices, although Samuel Taylor Coleridge, another of the first generation Romantics, most certainly did not like the novel. Coleridge, who often spoke very admiringly of Scott's works, in particular his poetry, disliked the novel because it was too mainstream and too popular; no thought was required to enjoy it, as he said in a letter to an associate:

Walter Scott's poems and novels (except only the two wretched abortions, *Ivanhoe* and *The Bride of Ravensmuir*, or whatever its name may be) supply both instance and solution of the present conditions and components of popularity, viz. to amuse without requiring any effort, and without exciting any deep emotion.

Coleridge is being deliberately disrespectful of Scott's *The Bride of Lammermoor* (1819) by misquoting its title, such is the contempt he obviously had for these works. While Romantic poets often claimed to want to reconnect mankind with poetry, having viewed eighteenth-century classicist poetry, of the type written by Winstanley, Pope, Addison, and the other leading lights of the Georgian era as too elitist. In practice, however, the poetry of the Romantics was arguably more elitist, and there was a lot snobbery from Romantic poets towards readers. They often saw themselves as being especially gifted and that it was only they whose inner souls manifested a poetic genius. Readers were supposed to read the works of Romantic poets and ponder deeper questions relating to nature and the self. Therefore, a novel such as *Ivanhoe* was viewed by Coleridge, who at this point in his life had turned a little bit cantankerous, which likely stemmed from his years of opium addiction, as something too cheap and sensational to spur men's thinking on to deeper issues. This attitude was repeated a few years later when Coleridge again criticised Scott's novel because it retold a story of two warring factions, the Saxons and the Normans. How much better *Ivanhoe* would have been, mused Coleridge, had Scott depicted the struggle between men of arms and men of arts in the medieval period! As interesting to a poet as Coleridge's suggestion would have been, Scott, however, knew that he was writing for a large readership in order to make money. Of course, had Coleridge actually read *Ivanhoe* from the beginning to the end, he might have had a different opinion. During the 1820s, he wrote to a friend that,

> I do not know myself how to account for it, but so the fact is, that tho' I have read, again and again turned to, sundry chapters of *Ivanhoe* with an untired interest, I have never read the whole … I never have been able to summon fortitude to read through.

Coleridge's comments on *Ivanhoe* and *The Bride of Lammermoor* were published in the press during the 1820s and 1830s. Yet Scott, in further proof of how much of an amiable man he was, did not hold a grudge and spoke very admiringly of Coleridge in later life, referring to him as 'that extraordinary man Coleridge' in 1828.

Readers did not have to wait long for another Robin Hood novel, for soon after Thomas Love Peacock published *Maid Marian* (1822). Peacock's novel is Marian's breakthrough and after its publication she would always be

Robin Hood's love interest. Peacock's novel was intended as a satire upon continental conservative governments. To fully understand his text, we must pause to consider the political context. According to a note which was inscribed on the fly leaf of the first edition of *Maid Marian*, Peacock began writing his novel in 1818. During the wars, Napoleon had installed some members of his family to rule France's European client states: Joseph Bonaparte ruled Spain between 1808 and 1813; Joachim Murat ruled over southern Italy between 1808 and 1811; Napoleon, of course, served as Emperor of France. After the war, with Napoleon defeated, the representatives of the allied forces at the Congress of Vienna insisted upon the restoration of *ancien regime* rulers in states that had been under the dominion of the Napoleonic Empire. While radicals and revolutionaries in some of these countries had managed to bring about some reforms, when the pre-Napoleonic rulers were restored they sought to dispense with any reforms that had been achieved during the wars. In Spain, for example, the liberal Constitution of 1812 was dispensed with by the newly restored Ferdinand VII who decided that he would rule as an absolute monarch instead. It seemed as though feudalism and despotism were returning to the continent.

Unlike the Tory, Scott, who argues in *Ivanhoe* that feudalism can be adapted to solve the political and social crises of the present, Peacock takes the opposite view and argues that the aristocratic and monarchical elites have always been greedy, self-interested, and violent towards the working and middle classes. Consequently, if there was to be any hope of political reform it needed to come from middle-class people who shared common goals with the working classes. These sentiments would likely have been approved of by Peacock's circle of friends: Romantic and largely bourgeois radicals such as the unashamed democrat, Percy Bysshe Shelley, his wife, Mary Shelley, and, of course, Lord Byron. Yet, paradoxically, while Peacock's novel can be read as a vehement criticism of the nobility, he still portrays Robin Hood as a nobleman. Scott, on the other hand, portrays him as a member of the working classes. In fact, Peacock's portrayal of Robin and Marian was one of the most 'lordly' to have yet appeared: Robin and Marian are described figuratively as 'King and Queen of the Forest', while Little John and Will Scarlet are the 'Peers of the Forest' who assist Robin and Marian in administering natural justice to the poor and oppressed.

In terms of plot, there is nothing in *Maid Marian* that is particularly innovative or noteworthy. All that Peacock does is adapt the stories of some of the better-known tales of Robin Hood that appeared in seventeenth-century ballads, along with some new material and a siege that is reminiscent of the one that occurs in *Ivanhoe*. Where the novel did break new ground was in its depiction of Maid Marian as a headstrong and independent, almost proto-feminist leading lady and inspired by Mary Shelley and her mother, Mary Wollstonecraft, the author of *A Vindication of the Rights of Woman* (1792). Thus, we see that Marian is no delicate little lady: she defies the wishes of her father, who seeks to confine her to the domestic sphere, by joining Robin in the forest and living the life of an outlaw. Once she becomes an outlaw and goes to live in the forest, she takes an active role in defending Sherwood from the depredations of the Sheriff. Such proto-feminist depictions of Maid Marian would be followed by some later Victorian authors as well as more recent filmmakers.

Upon its first publication, reviewers seemed to like *Maid Marian*. It was commended for its 'plot, incident, strongly-marked characters and good language' in *The Literary Chronicle*. Scott's work was more popular, however: *Ivanhoe* went through numerous editions and has never been out of print, unlike Peacock's novel which went through only one edition, was revived briefly in the 1830s, and then again in the late nineteenth century. Several stage plays of *Ivanhoe* also appeared at theatres throughout the country and at one point four plays were running concurrently in London, with each showing a different part of the plot. The idea was that patrons could view the story of *Ivanhoe* in sequence. Even when *Maid Marian* was adapted for the stage, its plot was often merged with *Ivanhoe*, as happened in James Robinson Planché's *Maid Marian; or, The Huntress of Arlingford* (1822). Peacock's novel thus lives in the shadow of Scott's *Ivanhoe*.

Chapter 6

The Victorian Period

A cheer for Robin Hood
And Nottingham's famed wood;
When the greensward was the merry men's resort:
When the tough and springy yew,
Was the bravest tree that grew,
And the Bow held foremost place in English sport.

Eliza Cook, *The Bow* (1870)

Long live Richard, Robin and Richard!
Long live Richard! Down with John!
Drink to the Lion-heart, Every-one!

Alfred, Lord Tennyson, *The Foresters* (1892)

With Walter Scott's *Ivanhoe* having in large part initiated the medieval revival of the 1820s, Victorian architects, artists, and authors began to turn back to the medieval period for inspiration. After the Houses of Parliament burned down in 1834, a competition was launched for designers to formulate plans for the new Houses of Parliament. The winning design was not a classical one, but one which evoked the medieval and early modern period with a gothic façade. In 1839, Lord Archibald Eglington held a medieval-themed jousting tournament at his estate, which dignitaries from far and wide attended, dressed as medieval heroes. The jousting event itself was inspired by the one which occurs in Scott's novel. The typical Scottish weather dampened the proceedings somewhat but the fact that the event was held signalled an enthusiasm for an idealised medieval past among Victorian elites. In spite of the fact that tournaments such as the one held Eglington evoked a primarily aristocratic view of the medieval past the Victorians, paradoxically, loved Robin Hood as a result of Scott's portrayal of him as the yeoman freedom fighter in *Ivanhoe*. In fact, from c. 1838 onwards there was a proliferation of Robin Hood literature.

Many of the novelists discussed in this chapter portray Robin Hood as an anti-Norman, Anglo-Saxon freedom fighter due to the influence of Scott's novel. The idea came to be regarded as an undisputed fact in the Victorian era. The French historian Augustin Thierry, in *The History of the Norman Conquest* (1825), wrote that 'Robin Hood [was] the last chief of outlaws or Anglo-Saxon bandits'. Henry Walter's *A History of England* (1828) similarly stated that Robin Hood was 'of Saxon blood; and the people wished him well, because they heard that he was a thorn in the side of the Norman gentry dwelling, or passing, near his abode in Sherwood Forest'. Even John Mathew Gutch, a serious scholar, assumed that Robin Hood was likewise of Anglo-Saxon heritage. Scott's novel was so well-researched, which was complete with footnotes, that very few people thought to question his idea. Further references to Robin Hood's Anglo-Saxon heritage are found in historical scholarship throughout the Victorian period. As there was in the Victorian period a scholarly consensus around the idea of Robin's Anglo-Saxon heritage as a confirmed fact, it was only natural that the following Victorian authors, who wished to be 'historically accurate', should draw upon the idea. The portrayal of Robin Hood as an Anglo-Saxon is also found in twentieth-century portrayals of the legend. Even today in Sherwood Forest's visitor centre, the life-size mannequin of Robin Hood speaks to visitors as they enter, and tells them of how 'I became an outlaw when the Normans took my land'. In fact, it is only in late twentieth-century and twenty-first-century movies that the idea is seemingly abandoned, for Scott's idea appears nowhere in *Robin Hood: Prince of Thieves* (1991), the BBC's *Robin Hood* (2006–09), or *Robin Hood* (2010).

Thomas Miller's *Royston Gower; or, The Days of King John* was published in 1838. Miller was born in Gainsborough, Lincolnshire in 1807. His father died when he was very young as a result of having participated in the Burdett Riots in 1810, leaving Miller and his mother in desperate poverty. Despite the dire straits that the family were reduced to, however, Miller's mother ensured that he received an education. From an early age he loved to read, and went on to become a poet and novelist. As far as his literary works go, he appears to have been a 'Jack of all trades'. His output ranged from pastoral poetry, to historical romance, to crime fiction.

Scott's *Ivanhoe* is clearly Miller's model and he pays homage to Scott in the preface, but he is not conservative like his literary hero, for in Miller's novel, we see an unfit king supported by a corrupt establishment composed of scheming nobles and decadent bishops. Miller is also unafraid to make direct comparisons between the thirteenth-century establishment and early Victorian politicians. The timing of the novel's publication in 1838 is significant as it coincided with the beginnings of the Chartist movement. As we saw earlier, during the eighteenth and nineteenth centuries, neither the middle classes nor the working classes had the vote. After much political agitation, the vote was extended to affluent members of the middle classes, being those who either owned or leased property worth forty shillings, landowners with copyhold land over £10, and tenants who paid an annual rent of £50. This of course left the working classes in the lurch; their previous allies in the cause of parliamentary reform – the middle classes – had abandoned them because they had achieved their own goals. Then with the support of the middle classes, the political establishment began passing laws which seemed intent on hurting the destitute, notably the Poor Law Amendment Act (1834) which expanded the workhouse system. Thus a new campaign for political reform was created by six working men and six MPs. They drew up a document called the People's Charter, and the name by which the movement would become known was Chartism. In its final form, it was a petition which included six demands: a vote for all working men; annual parliamentary elections; equal-sized constituencies; salaries for MPs; the secret ballot; and the abolition of the property requirement for people to become an MP.

Miller depicts Robin Hood as a yeoman from a humble station in life who, because of political oppression under the Normans, has been forced to become an outlaw. However, Robin Hood is not the main character in Miller's novel. Instead the focus is upon the title character, Royston, who is an Anglo-Saxon soldier in the pay of the Normans. However, when he learns that the Anglo-Saxons are petitioning King John to publicly support the implementation of a 'charter of rights' that seeks a vaguely defined idea of 'political enfranchisement' for the Anglo-Saxon serfs, he joins with the outlaws and assists them in their fight for political rights. Therefore, Robin Hood is not simply an outlawed yeoman but a political reformer, and is named as such in Miller's preface, albeit a reformer who is not afraid to resort to the use of physical force. 'Peaceably if we may, forcibly as we must', was one Chartist slogan adopted in 1839, a sentiment that is obviously echoed in Miller's text. Robin even assists in a small-scale peasants' revolt in Nottingham, which is led by a character named Hereward whom, although invoking the name of an eleventh-century outlaw, is obviously modelled upon the leader of the 1381 rebellion, Wat Tyler. Of course, a charter is granted at the end of the novel, but it is of little use to the common people.

Chartism never succeeded as movement in spite of the authorities' worries, and by c. 1850, the movement had ground to a halt in spite of having the support of some big names in the Victorian press such as the vehement radical, G. W. M. Reynolds (1814–79). As such, the end of *Royston Gower*, in which the government ignore the demands of the people and are still in thrall to serfdom and political oppression seems eerily prophetic. Although the actual Chartist movement never achieved its goals, however, all but one of their demands were enacted by successive governments. The right of some working men to vote was granted in 1867, and the franchise was extended to include all working men in 1918, along with some women. Working men could stand for election after the property qualification required to be an MP was abolished in 1857, although this did not initially improve working-class representation in Westminster because very few men could commit to the job when it was unpaid. In fact, MPs did not become salaried professionals until 1911. The Redistribution of Seats Act 1885 ensured that parliamentary constituencies would be, where possible, of an equal size. The secret ballot was guaranteed under the Ballot Act of 1870.

While Miller's novel, published in the three volume format like Scott's *Ivanhoe*, received some very positive reviews, the most successful Robin Hood text from the Victorian period, in commercial terms, was Pierce Egan the Younger's penny blood entitled *Robin Hood and Little John; or, The Merry Men of Sherwood Forest*, published between 1838 and 1840. He was the son of the more famous Pierce Egan, the Regency writer and sports journalist, often styled 'the Elder' (1772–1849), although very little is known of the younger Egan's early life. He first came to public notice when he provided the illustrations to a work that his father had written entitled *The Pilgrims of the Thames in Search of the National* (1838). After the *Pilgrims*, he turned his attention to writing and published his first novel *Quintin Matsys: The Blacksmith of Antwerp* in the latter half of 1838, at the end of which he also began writing *Robin Hood*, for which he provided the illustrations.

Penny bloods, and their successors the penny dreadfuls, were inexpensive serialised novels, often anonymously authored, which appeared in weekly instalments and marketed primarily towards the working and lower-middle classes. The stories were melodramatic, and were filled with sex and violence, and the stories were often adapted from those which appeared in expensive three volume novels. Henry Downes Miles's penny blood *Dick Turpin the Highwayman* (1845), for instance, is almost identical in its plot to William Harrison Ainsworth's *Rookwood* (1834). The highwayman, Dick Turpin (1705–1739), was a penny dreadful 'hero', inspiring the popular *Black Bess, or the Knight of the Road*, a story of mammoth length that was published between 1866 and 1868. The penny blood was not a marginal genre of literature, however, as novelists such as Egan sold novels 'by the half-million'. One of Egan's friends, G. W. M. Reynolds, authored *The Mysteries of London* (1844–48), which was one of the most widely read and bestselling novels of the Victorian era.

Egan's *Robin Hood* begins by paying homage to Joseph Ritson: a character bearing his surname delivers an orphaned foundling to the cottage of Gilbert Hood, who is a Forester living in Sherwood. Secrecy surrounds Robin's birth but it eventually transpires that he is the heir to the Earldom of Huntingdon. Gilbert raises Robin Hood to be a tough yet chivalrous young Saxon man who is ever ready to come to the aid of the oppressed. The Saxon and Norman racialism is subtly present in the novel, although in terms of plot it is relatively meaningless and is referred to only sporadically throughout. In fact, Egan's Robin Hood, after he is elected as leader of the outlaws, aims to be the hero of both the poor Saxons and poor Normans. This Robin Hood, therefore, aims to be the hero *of* the people – that is, of *all people* whatever their ethnicity. Egan's personal politics were radical, and all of his early novels, especially *Wat Tyler* (1841), subtly advocated for democracy and a healthy distrust of the political establishment.

Although Miller and Egan portrayed Robin Hood as a man with Chartist and radical sympathies, there are surprisingly very few references to be found of Robin Hood in the archives of the Victorian radical press. There are a few grumblings about the aristocracy, in both the past and present that can be found in radical publications such as *Reynolds's Newspaper*, in which a writer called Gracchus argued that,

> Servile historians have depicted as robbers, rascals, and freebooters men who were in reality doing their utmost to save themselves and posterity from being plundered by the ancestors of those coroneted robbers who now hold possession of a large portion of English soil.

The choice of the author's pseudonym is telling, for he evidently wants to be associated with the Roman popular leader, Tiberius Gracchus

(c. 169–133 BC). The author evidently believes that history writing has, until his day, been whitewashed and skewed in favour of the elites. But even towards the end of century, there are only passing references to Robin Hood in socialist periodicals. There would not be a specific socialist-inspired portrayal of the Robin Hood story until Geoffrey Trease published *Bows Against the Barons* (1934).

In terms of plot, Egan's novel is a melodrama in prose. There is a comically nasty villain in the Sheriff of Nottingham, or Baron Fitzalwine, prone to fits of violent outbursts, often punishing his own guards and screaming lines such as 'I shall exterminate them all!' The sheriff's rage towards his men is often justified, however, because his guards are quite inept in their duties; Robin seems to come and go from Nottingham castle just as he pleases and is never caught. The outlaws are also capable of almost superhuman feats, especially when a small number of them fight off a Norman army who has come looking for them in the forest. There are also plenty of 'Victorian' damsels in distress who often faint at the most critical points to enhance the suspense, one of these being when the outlaws are being pursued by the sheriff's men in the vaults of the castle, in obvious echoes of Horace Walpole's *The Castle of Otranto* (1764). In fact, the sheriff himself likewise recalls the rather unhinged baron, Manfred, in Walpole's novel. And in the novel, such scenes are narrated in a suitably dramatic way, such as when Allen-a-Dale's fiancée is escaping from a Norman through the forest and Egan exclaims, 'Holy Mother! She has swooned! This is an awkward predicament!' One does have to wonder whether, in his representation of female fragility, Egan was satirising the figure of the delicate Victorian 'Angel in the House' type of woman that was idealised during the Victorian era.

At a time when violent entertainment was slowly being outlawed by the predominantly upper-middle-class establishment in an effort to curb what they saw as unwholesome working-class recreations, and thereby impose bourgeois ideals of respectability upon the working classes, the novel had the right ingredients to satisfy working- and lower-middle class readers' appetites for violent entertainment. Plenty of Norman soldiers' limbs get cut off, arrows are sent shooting through people's eyes. Maid Marian suffers two attempted rapes at the hands of Norman soldiers, and after the second attempt Robin slays the would-be perpetrator and hangs his mangled body on a tree in the forest as a warning to any others who might think of committing a similar crime. Robin even burns a guard's eyes with a torch in order to allow him and his men to escape from the castle at one point. Guy of Gisborne meets his death in the same manner as the early ballad narrates it, with his head cut off and his face mutilated. Yet, readers should not flinch from such gratuitous displays of violence, argues Egan, for the medieval period was a violent time and so the brutality of the novel should not bother readers. In spite of Egan's justification for the violence of his novel, reviewers were not impressed. Egan's works, as well as those of his friend Reynolds, were often criticised in the press. One reviewer in *The Times* remarked that the content of both of these writers' works can be summed up using two words: lust and murder.

As an appendix to the first edition of Egan's novel, published in 1840, which included all of the penny parts, Egan included an anthology of Robin Hood ballads. Egan's ballad collection is based upon eighteenth-century versions of *Robin Hood's Garland*. These were anthologies of seventeenth-century Robin Hood ballads, although it is only the early modern ballads included in Egan's collection, such as *Robin Hood and the Tanner, Robin Hood and the Jolly Pinder of Wakefield, Robin Hood and Allen-a-Dale*, and *Robin Hood and the Bishop of Hereford*. The medieval poems such as *A Gest of Robyn Hode* and *Robin Hood and the Monk* are, strangely, not included in Egan's version, even though they were, by the 1840s, well known as a result of Ritson's ballad anthology having being reprinted several times. The extent of Egan's actual 'editing' of these texts was minimal. The decision to include a ballad collection as an appendix was perhaps the publisher George Pierce's idea. The preface included at the beginning is virtually plagiarised from Charles Johnson's eighteenth-century account of Robin Hood, with one or two notes from Ritson inserted towards the end. One contribution to the ballad collection that we can tell Egan did make, however, is in the illustrations he provided (he had also provided all of the images for the novel in the first edition). Through his images, he provided continuity with his preceding novel because the characters of Robin Hood and his men who appear in the novel look exactly the same as those which appear in this ballad collection.

Egan's novel was so popular that it went through at least six editions throughout the nineteenth century, although very few of them after c. 1850 retain the ballad anthology as an appendix. The novel was then adapted for a French audience by Alexandre Dumas in two novels entitled *Le Prince des Voleurs* (1872) and *Robin de Bois* (1873). These were then translated back into English as *The Prince of Thieves* and *Robin Hood the Outlaw* in the early twentieth century by Alfred Allinson. One novel was somewhat eclipsed by the success of Egan's: Stephen Percy's *Tales of Robin Hood* (1840). Percy's is the first book-length Robin Hood story that was written specifically for children. There had of course been some children's stories of Robin Hood published before this, notably in *Tabart's Collection of Popular Stories for the Nursery* (1805–09), which was edited by the popular eighteenth-century novelist, William Godwin. Unsurprisingly, Tabart's version is very conservative, as illustrated in the following passage:

> Though Robin Hood was a robber, which, to be sure, is not bad thing, he behaved himself in such a manner as to have the good word and good wishes of all the neighbourhood. He never loved to rob anyone except people who were very rich, and who had not lived to make good use of their riches.

Tabart's sets the tone for the later Victorian children's books which were to be published by Percy, and then later in the nineteenth-century by various authors.

There were other penny bloods that were published after Egan which attempted to capitalise upon Egan's success, notably J. H. Stocqueler who wrote *Maid Marian, the Forest Queen; Being a Companion to 'Robin Hood'* (1849). Stocqueler's novel allegedly takes place in the same universe as Egan's, for the title is meant to imply that *Maid Marian* is not only a companion to Robin Hood in terms of its principal character being Robin Hood's wife, but that the text is a companion to Egan's *Robin Hood*. The adventures related by Stocqueler are supposed to take place at some unspecified point in Egan's narrative. However, apart from the title, there is little in terms of plot that actually connects Stocqueler's novel to Egan's story in his actual text.

Stocqueler sets his story, as most Victorian authors do, during the 1190s. The novel is noteworthy because it is the first time that we see a Robin Hood story begin in the Holy Land. Robin is away on Crusade, having been conscripted as a punishment from King Richard for being an outlaw. And it is through his introductory chapters that Stocqueler really shows off his experience as a travel writer, for the novel is rich in orientalist descriptions of the people and places of the Middle East. The novel is also noteworthy because it is the first time in a Robin Hood story that a Muslim character returns with Robin to join his outlaw band and fight against the Norman authorities. Similar stories would be followed in *Robin of Sherwood*, *Robin Hood: Prince of Thieves*, and the BBC's *Robin Hood*. While Robin is absent,

Marian has been in left in charge of the outlaws in Sherwood Forest. Prince John lusts after her and sends one of his men into the forest to abduct her. After a brave fight against her kidnapper, she is eventually overcome and carried off to Nottingham castle, which requires the outlaws to rescue her. Robin then returns and reassumes control of the outlaws, and the narrative ceases to have any originality but simply copies *Ivanhoe*, with some of the dialogue copied almost verbatim from Scott's novel. There is a jousting tournament where Robin rescues one Wilfrid of Cotherstone, a character obviously based upon Wilfrid of Ivanhoe. There is also a spectacular siege against a castle held by some bad French Knights Templar, as happens in Scott's novel.

While Stocqueler initiated the storyline, common to many portrayals of Robin Hood in our era, that the outlaw was a crusader and brought back a Muslim ally to help him in his struggle against the corrupt sheriff, the novel did not have a big impact when it was first published. The same goes for the anonymously authored *Little John and Will Scarlet* (1865), which practically regurgitates the plot of Egan's story. *Little John and Will Scarlet* is interesting, however, because as its title suggests it focuses upon Robin's comrades and their female companions, and is filled with the usual amounts of violence. In a similar manner to Egan's novel, the author was also an advocate of republican politics, at one point saying that it would have been better for England had Oliver Cromwell's vision of a republican nation in the seventeenth century succeeded. Although Egan himself was a passionate advocate of radical politics and a friend to the Chartists, he never criticised the British monarchy.

While Egan and Reynolds walked a fine line between respectability and vulgarity, penny dreadfuls came in for an excessive amount of condemnation by moralists in the Victorian press. The following comment from a late-Victorian reviewer is fairly typical of how the genre was viewed by many:

> There is now before us such a veritable mountain of pernicious trash, mostly in paper covers, and 'Price One Penny'; so-called novelettes, tales, stories of adventure, mystery and crime; pictures of school life hideously unlike reality; exploits of robbers, cut-throats, prostitutes, and rogues, that, but for its actual presence, it would seem incredible.

Penny dreadfuls were popular with both younger and more mature readers. Eighteenth-century criminals such as Jack Sheppard and Dick Turpin usually featured as their heroes, but there were quite a few medieval tales also published as penny numbers, including many Robin Hood stories. Sometimes they were issued as standalone periodicals, such as George Emmett's *Robin Hood and the Archers of Merrie Sherwood* (1868–69), but more often than not a few chapters per week were featured in magazines such as *The Boys of England*. It was in this publication that a long-running serial entitled *The Prince of Archers, or, The Boyhood Days of Robin Hood* first appeared in 1883.

Emmett's novel begins promisingly by setting the story of Robin Hood, not during the times of King Richard and Prince John, but during Simon de Montfort's rebellion which occurred between 1264 and 1267. The new setting had been attempted in a novel published previously in the century: G. P. R. James's *Forest Days* (1843), in which Robin likewise joins de Montfort's side. James's novel was unremarkable and made little impact in the Victorian press or upon subsequent portrayals of Robin. In any case, it is de Montfort who is the real hero in James's novel and Robin is simply an outlaw who decides to join the fight. Emmett was not as talented a writer as James was, but his Robin Hood novel was immensely popular with young lads and went through several reprints. Neither its text nor its images are historicised. In the illustrations, Robin is always dressed more as a seventeenth-century highwayman than a medieval outlaw. The publisher probably reused or adapted some of the images from other stories to furnish Emmett's novel. This was fairly common practice in some cheap publications. As is usual in the later Victorian penny dreadfuls, Robin is the Earl of Huntingdon although in other places, Emmett also calls Robin a yeoman, a change for which Emmet does not account. The one interesting insertion into the narrative is that of the Forest Demon. When Robin and his men are outlawed for joining Simon de Montfort in his rebellion, they make their home in Sherwood Forest. It is here that Robin meets the strange woodland creature. Forest spirits would make their way into further Robin Hood adaptations such as Paul Creswick's *Robin Hood and his Adventures* (1917) and in the television series *Robin of Sherwood* (1984–86). The association between Robin Hood and woodland spirits comes from a now discredited theory from the 1830s (which was never taken seriously at the time anyway), referred to in the introduction, that supposed Robin to be the manifestation of the Teutonic woodland spirit Hodekin. This idea subsequently made it into *The Oxford Dictionary of National Biography* when Sir Sidney Lee was editing the first edition of it during the late nineteenth century.

THE VICTORIAN PERIOD

As the title of *The Prince of Archers; or, The Young Lord of Huntingdon* suggests, it is the story of Robin's youth. Robin and his father live on the Huntingdon estate, but the political rival of the Lord of Huntingdon is the Lord of Torilstone who lives not far from the Huntingdons. Readers familiar with Scott's work will immediately recognise the not-so-subtle similarity to Torquilstone in *Ivanhoe*. Other similarities to *Ivanhoe* are the fact that one of the key villains in *The Young Lord of Huntingdon* is Sir Front de Boeuf, who is a villain in both novels. There are also racial tensions between the Saxons and the Normans, which is usual in Victorian Robin Hood narratives that relied heavily on Scott. After Robin's family estates are confiscated by Prince John, Robin and Little John are forced to seek shelter in Sherwood Forest. They come across some outlaws and, upon learning that he is of noble birth, they ask him to become their leader. Instead of being elected as leader of the outlaws in Egan's novel, Robin is 'appointed King of Sherwood'. Obviously there is a subtle message here that, in typical Victorian fashion, the working classes need the upper classes to lead them, and those at the bottom of the heap should likewise defer to their 'betters'. Robin does steal from the rich and give to the poor, but this is done by the outlaws more out of a sense of Christian charity and is not a political mission. On the face of it, this appears to be respectable reading. But before we assume that this story was considered as wholesome reading for youths, it should be noted that the narrative is filled with graphic descriptions and illustrations of violence. Here is an example of the cruelty of one of the Norman Barons to their servants:

> 'Base Slave!' thundered the Baron; and then with all the force of his muscular arm, he brought down the heavy drinking cup upon the skull of the soldier who stood uncovered before him. The wretched man fell to the ground and lay senseless, bleeding from a terrible scalp wound; the tankard was crushed and bent out of shape by the force of the blow.

There is also an attempted rape upon the sweetheart of Allen-a-Dale. The outrages of the Normans are met with an equally violent response by the outlaws. Robin and his men do not hesitate to resort to violence. This is the description of Robin shooting one of Baron Torilstone's retainers through the eye: 'the missile flew true to its mark, its steel point entering the man's eye, pierced his brain'. While many Victorians in general quietly enjoyed violent entertainment, there were limits as to how much would be tolerated in the public arena. The violence contained in the stories published by *The Boys of England* led to it being widely condemned in the press as an example of the pernicious reading that was used as a scapegoat for what appeared to be, according to some rather alarmed commentators in the Victorian press, was the cause of an ever-rising tide of juvenile crime.

Individual stories from *The Boys of England* were rarely picked up on, usually because its critics never bothered to read them. There were many instances in court when the magazine appeared in the dock. In 1872, in the trial of a 13-year-old boy who was indicted for murdering a family member confessed that he had been reading *The Boys of England* which had caused him to commit the crime. Policemen and journalists usually made sure to point out whether a particular juvenile offender had on his person at the time of his arrest a copy of a penny dreadful. When a 13-year-old was arrested for stealing £7 from his father, *The Times* reported that 'his pockets were crammed with copies of *The Pirates League*, or *The Seagull*, the *Young Briton*, *Sons of Britannia* and *The Boys of England*'. Thus, to moral crusaders it seemed straightforward: reading penny dreadful tales really did turn working-class youngsters into criminals. For example, a headmaster in 1874 wrote that:

> The hero in these periodicals, read openly in the streets, devoured, I should say, by the thousands of errand and work boys, is he who defies his governors, teachers, spiritual pastors and masters, and is the leader of the most outrageous acts.

Penny dreadfuls were in fact a convenient scapegoat for the rise in juvenile crime among working-class boys for sanctimonious middle-class journalists to pass on their concerns to their readers. This effectively absolved the Victorian upper classes of any responsibility for making living conditions better for working-class children; these boys did not turn to crime because they were poor, even if research has shown that most petty theft in the Victorian period was due to poverty, but because their morals had been corrupted by bad entertainment.

While penny dreadfuls were viewed as unwholesome reading, at the same time a number of 'five shilling' conservative children's books were published, in part to offset the supposed pernicious effects of popular penny literature. Young people in ever greater numbers were, in the latter part of the Victorian period, able to read after the passage of the Education Act (1870), which required all children to learn the basics of reading, writing, and arithmetic. In many of these children's books, it is a young boy who is the hero. This was a standard format followed by many late nineteenth-century children's writers, such as G. A. Henty. His stories usually followed the adventures of a local boy who enlists in the army and ends up serving under the command of some imperial hero such as Robert Clive (1725–74). Although they were intended as books which both working-class and middle-class boys could read, in terms of their content, they were often very bourgeois and suited to public school boys. Edward Gilliat's *In Lincoln Green: A Story of Robin Hood* (1897) is a prime example of this. It follows the adventures of Robin's son, Walter, heir to the Earldom of Huntingdon, who is enrolled at a local public school. Gilliat himself was the Assistant Headmaster of Harrow. Unbeknownst to Walter, his father is the famous outlaw, Robin Hood. The rivalry between Robin and the Sheriff is reflected in the playground scraps that ensue with the school bully, Master Malapert, who happens to be the Sheriff's son. There are some painful jokes in the form of Latin puns, which, presumably, young male readers from public schools will have found amusing. Further books written in a similar, genteel style to Gilliat's novel were published into the Edwardian era. In all of them, Robin Hood is the Earl of Huntingdon and also a Saxon, in what was fast becoming a tired narrative trope, especially as many of them virtually lift certain scenes from *Ivanhoe*.

It would be wrong for us to assume that Robin Hood was merely a hero for radicals or simply confined to the realm of children's books, because Robin Hood was entering into the drawing room in an entirely different form. Adults could even purchase a figurine of Robin Hood to adorn their fire places. During the nineteenth century, Staffordshire emerged as one of the leading regions in Britain for the production of ceramics and pottery. A number of potters in the region began to turn their hands to producing commemorative figures of famous people in the 1830s and 1840s. Some of these included statues of the Duke of Wellington and various other political figures. By the 1860s, Staffordshire potters' figurine range was expanded to include royal figures, historical personalities, sportsmen, and even criminals. The eighteenth-century thief, Dick Turpin, was a popular figurine, as was the Italian freedom fighter, Giuseppe Garibaldi. It was during the 1860s that a figurine of Robin Hood and Little John first appeared for sale. The actual figures are attired in costumes that, with their breeches and tunics, look more like they were from the early modern period rather than the medieval period. Most of the surviving ornaments were produced in the 'flatback' style in order to be placed upon a mantelpiece, and presumably their purchasers will have placed them there to have pride of place in the home. Thus, Robin Hood could be anti-establishment for some people and conservative for others; this really was a period in which Robin Hood could be appropriated by anybody for any purpose.

In the realm of Victorian high theatre, Robin Hood was fast becoming a nationalist hero by virtue of his allegedly Saxon birth. The composer, George Macfarren, along with the dramatist John Oxenford, turned their hands to the outlaw's story and wrote a highly successful opera entitled *Robin Hood*, which premiered at Her Majesty's Theatre in 1860, which was staged over two seasons and also enjoyed a successful nationwide tour. It is clearly an opera which is meant to inspire pride in Englishmen's Anglo-Saxon heritage, as illustrated by the following song which Robin sings:

> *Locksley.* Englishmen by birth are free;
> Though their limbs you chain,
> Glowing thoughts of liberty,
> In their hearts remain.
> Normans do whate'er you can,
> Ne'er you'll crush the Englishman!
>
> *Chorus.* Normans do whate'er you can,
> Ne'er you'll crush the Englishman!
>
> *Locksley.* Our fathers were of Saxon race,
> With Hengist here they came;
> And when they found this resting place,
> They lit a sacred flame.
> It did not blaze from alter or from pyre;
> But burning in the English heart is still that deathless fire!
>
> *Chorus.* Englishmen by birth are free, &c.
>
> *Locksley.* The deathless flame of liberty
> We prize a treasure dear;
> Though hidden for a while it be,
> At length 'twill reappear.
> In vain our proud oppressors seek,
> The Saxon race to quell;
> Their bonds of iron are but weak,
> While freedom in the soul can dwell.

Pride in the accomplishments of the Anglo-Saxon 'race' would eventually, especially after the publication of Charles Darwin's *On the Origin of Species* (1859), give way to a general feeling that English people were racially superior to the indigenous people of their empire. This ideology was known as Social Darwinism, and it was often used by the ideologues of the British Empire as a justification for imperial expansion; the superiority of English people seemed self-evident, after all, for they had become masters of the world by the second half of the nineteenth century; they held themselves to be more 'civilised' and they should therefore aim to spread their own civilisation throughout the world. At the end of Macfarren's play, Richard I returns and pardons Robin Hood, and the sheriff, whose daughter is Maid Marian, consents for the outlaw and Marian to finally get married. Yet once they are married, Robin is duty-bound to serve his country abroad, which no doubt would have been seen by contemporary audiences as the equivalent of nineteenth-century imperial service:

> *Sheriff.* The warrant for this outlaw's death I bring [...] 'The acts of violence committed by the bold outlaw, commonly called Robin Hood, have reached our ear; his constant defiance of the law merits the severest punishment, and he would be utterly unworthy of pardon were not his deeds to be ascribed in some measure to the misgovernment of our brother, John, and his nefarious agents. As the country is in want of defenders against threatening foes, we hereby offer to Robin Hood and all his comrades, on condition that they employ their well-tried valour in the country's service, a free pardon.'
>
> *Robin.* Gladly I'll fight for my country and king;
> At last they're united – their cause is the same.
>
> *Chorus.* We'll die to a man, for the lion-hearted king.

Stephen Knight points out that imperial ideology finds its way into other late nineteenth-century Robin Hood plays such as Alfred, Lord Tennyson's *The Foresters* (1892), with its references to the sun which never sets. Contained within the play is the usual nationalist sycophancy for Richard I:

> Now the King is home again, and nevermore to roam again.
> Now the King is home again, the King will have his own again,

Home again, home again, and each will have his own again,
All the birds in merry Sherwood sing and sing him home again.

Tennyson's play opened in America and enjoyed moderate success but was heavily criticised in Britain when it opened for being too childlike, and some modern critics have been more scathing about the play's lack of literary or artistic merit.

The most prominent association between Robin Hood, nationalism, and the British Empire, however, could be seen when people dressed as Robin Hood at Empire Day pageants. This was a commemorative day which was first celebrated on 24 May 1901 throughout the whole of the British Empire. At these events, adults and especially children were encouraged to don costumes of historical figures from English history. The event was intended to instil pride in the historical achievements of the nation; streets would be decked out in union-flag bunting and songs such as *Rule Britannia* and *God Save the King* were sung by local choirs. Yet it was not only patriotic songs that were sung at these events, for folk songs could be heard too, and early modern Robin Hood songs were a part of this corpus of national songs which local organisers had at their disposal. Related to such imperial events were scouting pageants, in which boys would often dress up as historical figures for parades. As a man who lived in the forest, Robin Hood was an ideal role model for young scouts, who were taught survivalist skills in the outdoors. These skills would toughen them up and turn them into 'manly' men, ready to serve the British Empire, in accordance with the pro-imperial ideology of its founder, Robert Baden-Powell, especially as seen in his book entitled *Young Knights of Empire* (1917). The appropriation of Robin Hood for an imperial cause was often an awkward fit compared to how the legend had thus far developed, however, because most of the previous portrayals actually criticise English rulers for pursuing overseas adventures and leaving England to rot.

Many of the late-Victorian portrayals of Robin Hood draw inspiration from Scott's novel by rehashing the nationalist theme of conflict between the Anglo-Saxons and the Normans. A breath of fresh air from this tired trope came in the form of Howard Pyle's *The Merry Adventures of Robin Hood* (1883) because Pyle went back to the stories of seventeenth-century ballads and out of them fashioned an exciting and engaging narrative. Unlike the novels which had gone before, Pyle's work was not intended as a political, moral, or social commentary, but was simply supposed to be enjoyed for its own sake. The work opens with the following admonition, stating that boring, overly serious people should not bother reading the book:

> You who so plod amid serious things that you feel it shame
> to give yourself up even for a few short moments to mirth
> and joyousness in the land of fancy; you who think that life
> hath nought to do with innocent laughter that can harm no one;
> these pages are not for you.

Pyle begins his novel with retelling in prose the story of a ballad entitled *Robin Hood's Progress to Nottingham*, which tells the story of Robin Hood's first crime and how he became an outlaw. While on his way to an archery contest being held in the town, Robin is stopped by a group of foresters who taunt him about his age and say he is a terrible archer and much too young to compete in front of the king. To prove them wrong, one of the foresters tells him to kill a deer, which he does.

> 'Knowest thou not,' said another, 'that thou hast killed the
> king's deer, and, by the laws of our gracious lord and sovereign,
> King Harry, thine ears could be shaven close to thy head?'
> 'Catch him!' cried a third.
> 'Nay,' said a fourth, 'let him e'en go because of his tender years.'

Robin pays no attention to them and walks on, but he hears one of the foresters mutter an insult about him. Robin turns round and shoots an arrow into the man's head. One of the seventeenth-century versions actually depicts a more menacing young outlaw who proceeds to kill fourteen out of the fifteen foresters:

> Robin Hood hee took up his noble bow
> And his broad arrows all amain,
> And Robin he laught and began to smile,
> As he went over the plain.
>
> Then Robin Hood hee bent his noble bow,
> And his broad arrows he let flye,
> Till fourteen of his fifteen foresters,
> Upon the ground did lye.

Robin then turns to the forester who taunted him:

> He that did this quarrel first begin,
> Went tripping over the plain;
> But Robin he bent his noble bow,
> And he fetched him back again.
>
> You said I was no archer, said bold Robin Hood
> But say so now again,
> With that he sent another arrow,
> That split his head in twain.

In Pyle's novel, before the dead man's fellow foresters can apprehend young Robin, he disappears into the depths of the forest. The reason why Pyle chose to tone down the violence of this particular episode is unclear, for his book in other parts was no less violent than some of the widely-condemned penny dreadfuls, as we see in Pyle's retelling of Robin Hood's fight with Guy of Gisborne:

> Seeing that strength was going from [Guy], Robin leaped up and, quick as a flash, struck a back-handed blow beneath the sword arm. Down fell the sword from Guy of Gisborne's grasp, and back he staggered at the stroke, and, ere he could regain himself, Robin's sword passed through and through his body. Round he spun upon his heel, and, flinging his hands aloft with a shrill, wild cry, fell prone upon his face upon the green sod.

Pyle did not only write the story but also designed all of the illustrations which accompanied it. The designs were line drawings but they were highly detailed and depicted the most exciting parts of the novel. The work won praise from the socialist author and designer, William Morris (1834–96), who himself wrote several medieval-themed works for which he also provided the illustrations.

Robin Hood makes a fleeting appearance in Morris's *A Dream of John Ball* (1888), in which a time traveller arrives in Kent on the eve of the Peasants' Revolt and hears a 'a stave of Robin Hood' being sung in the village tavern before the arrival of John Ball. Morris actually composed his own entirely new Robin Hood ballad for the occasion. As the time traveller hears the song he says,

> My heart rose high as I heard him, for it was concerning the struggle against tyranny for the freedom of life, how that the wild wood and the heath, despite of wind and weather, were better for a free man than the court or the cheaping-town; of the taking from the rich to give to the poor; of the life of a man doing his own will and not the will of another man.

In an earlier article for the socialist newspaper, *Commonweal*, Morris and E. Belfort Bax argued that the roots of English socialist ideology and of commoners' resistance to the elites' property rights had their origins in tales of Robin Hood:

> Such, then, was the theory of Mediæval Society; but apart from whatever of oppression on life and thought was inherent [feudalism], the practice of the theory was liable to many abuses, to which the obvious confusion and misery of the times are mostly referable. These abuses again were met by a protest in the form of almost constant rebellion against Society, of which one may take as examples the organised vagabondage of Middle Europe, the Jacquerie in France, and in England what may be called the chronic rebellion of the Foresters, which produced such an impression on the minds of the people, that it has given birth to the ballad epic known by the name of its mythical hero, Robin Hood. Resistance to authority and contempt of the 'Rights of Property' are the leading ideas in this rough but noble poetry.

Morris, in linking the songs of Robin Hood to Wat Tyler, John Ball, and the 1381 rebellion, is attempting to reinject radical, anti-establishment ideas into the Robin Hood legend. There would not be a proper socialist portrayal of Robin Hood until the twentieth century, however, when Geoffrey Trease published *Bows Against the Barons* (1934). Trease wrote this book for children because he was frustrated with the prevailing conservative portrayals of Robin Hood that he had encountered in his youth and which were still being written. He felt that life in the greenwood in Victorian and Edwardian books was often too merry, showing little of the hardships which real outlaws would have endured. And as a socialist, he found the sycophantic ending of many Robin Hood tales, in which he blesses the king, to be totally at odds with what a real outlaw would have done, especially one who was the friend of the people. In a similar manner to Victorian children's novels, Robin Hood is not the main character in Trease's book, for it is a young serf called Dickon. Dickon's father has died and he must support his mother and sister. Hunger is a constant companion for the young man and his family, yet in spite of feeling weak from not being able to eat much, he suffers under the lash of the master's lieutenant if he is found to be tired in the field. One night, he is so hungry that almost without thinking he kills one of the king's deer. Knowing that this would mean certain death, he simply absconds from home and flees into Sherwood Forest. He shortly afterwards meets with Robin Hood and his men, who address each other as 'Comrades'. The outlaws mount two ultimately unsuccessful revolts against the local rulers, with echoes of Wat Tyler's rebellion, during which Much and Friar Tuck are killed. During Trease's narration of the revolt, there are references to peasants holding hammers and sickles, accompanied with illustrations, which were obviously meant to evoke images of the flag of the Soviet Union (interestingly, there were two Robin Hood films produced in the Soviet Union: *The Arrows of Robin Hood* in 1975 and *The Ballad of the Valiant Knight Ivanhoe* in 1983, although they only enjoyed a limited release in the west). At the end of the novel, Robin is also murdered by the Prioress of Kirklees, and Little John and Dickon flee to Derbyshire to continue the good fight against injustice.

At first glance, Robin Hood is the perfect socialist figure: he fights against corrupt rulers and redistributes wealth from the rich to the poor. It is very odd then that in the corpus of late-Victorian and early twentieth-century socialist writings there are very few references to Robin Hood. The truth is that Robin Hood was by the nineteenth century a socially conservative (small 'c') figure. Very few Robin Hood stories depict him as a man who wishes to completely overthrow the existing political order, unlike socialists desired at this point. Robin Hood's reputed loyalty to the king illustrates that he indeed has no problem at all with hierarchies. He will help out a poor person if he sees them in need, but that is the extent of his program. This is why Wat Tyler has always been favoured as a historical for socialists icon rather than Robin Hood, because the former, along with John Ball, had a program which aimed to improve the lives of commoners.

Additionally, Robin Hood was not the only greenwood outlaw featured in late-Victorian fiction, and he often served as a model for authors who wished to write tales of other medieval outlaws, so it is worth dwelling briefly upon Robert Louis Stevenson's *The Black Arrow* (1888). The prologue of the novel is quite sinister, opening with a mysterious outlaw shooting a man dead in a churchyard. Attached to the shaft is the following note:

I had four blak arrows under my belt,
Four for the greefs that I have felt,
Four for the number of ill menne,
That have opressid me now and then.
One is gone, one is wele sped,
Old Apulyard is ded.
One is for maister Bennet Hatch,
That burned Grimstone, walls and Thatch.
One for Sir Oliver Oates,
That cut Harry Shelton's throat.
Sir Daniel, ye shall have the fourt,
We shall think it fair sport.
Ye shull each have your own part,
A blak arrow in each blak heart.
Get ye to your knees for to pray:
Ye are ded theeves, by yea and nay!
John Amend-All. Of the Green Wood. And his Jolly Fellowship.

With his inclusion of John Amend-All, Stevenson is connecting his outlaws to the Jack Cade Rebellion, which was an alias used by the eponymous rebel in the rebellion of 1450.

There was an interesting ballad which appeared earlier in the nineteenth century entitled *Robin Hood's Courtship with Jack Cade's Daughter* (1822). The text was written by a Scottish antiquary named James Maidment but a few leading historians at the time were convinced that it was a newly discovered ancient ballad which, as its title implies, sees Robin Hood marry Joan Cade, the daughter of the famous rebel. The ballad is written in a feigned Old Scots, and this is the scene in which the pair declare their love for one another at the end:

Gif you luve me as you say,
You wad not leave this shade, sir;
Bot you wad live my Robin Hood,
And I your Joan Cade, sir.
Brume, brume, &c.

And I will nevir from ye part,
Bot live within this wode, oh!
An since you will be my Joan Cade,
Ise be your Robin Hood, oh!
Brume, brume, &c.

Even the serious scholar, J. M. Gutch, was thoroughly convinced by the text's alleged authenticity, remarking that the ballad 'upon the marriage of *Robin Hood and Jack Cade's Daughter* is a valuable relic, for its graceful simplicity and poetic imagery'. Obviously the text's lack of authenticity has been detected by later scholars, and in modern editions of Robin Hood texts *Robin Hood's Courtship with Jack Cade's Daughter* is clearly marked out as a forgery. Yet as Alex Kaufman says, when it comes to a figure such as Robin Hood, who has been reimagined and represented in a variety of different ways by various authors, nothing is 'real' as all texts, even dating back to the *Gest*, are pure fiction.

But to return to Stevenson's novel: as in most late-Victorian children's novels, the hero of the story is a young boy named Dick Shelton who has been raised by his protector, Sir Daniel, who turns out to be a villain who killed Dick's father some years earlier. The backdrop to the novel is the turbulent Wars of the Roses (1455–87). Obviously, outlaws and bandits have always flourished whenever and wherever there has been political turbulence, and apart from being outlaws, the novel at first glance has very little to do with Robin Hood. But there is a possibility that Stevenson intended it as a Robin Hood novel originally. In Stevenson's personal library was a copy of Jules Michelet's *Histoire de France* (1844). Michelet's history is unique in that it situates Robin and his merry men, not in the time of Richard I, a practice which had been popularised by Munday and Grafton, and practically every other author throughout history but, as Stevenson does in his novel, between 1455 and 1487. In speaking of Warwick the Kingmaker (a prominent figure in the wars), whom Stevenson's outlaws side with in his novel, Michelet writes that he was 'the King of the enemies of property, of the plunderers of the borders, and corsairs of the Strait'. Michelet then goes on to say that Robin Hood was one of Warwick's men:

> What is Robin Hood? The outlaw, Robin Hood, is naturally the enemy of the man of the law, the adversary of the Sheriff. In the long series of ballads of which he is the hero, we find him first inhabiting the green woods of Lincoln. He is induced to quit them by the French Wars, so he turns his back on the Sheriff and the King's deer, seeks the sea and crosses it [...] All Robin Hood's companions, all who were under ban of the law, were safe whilst Warwick (either personally or through his brother) was judge of the marches of Calais and Scotland.

It is this passage which Stevenson drew special attention to in his personal annotated copy of Michelet's text. Notwithstanding Michelet's highly suspect scholarship, Stevenson must have been convinced that the time of the wars between Lancaster and York was the perfect period in which to set an outlaw novel. The reason why he did not write a Robin Hood novel is probably because at this point the children's literature market was saturated with them. Furthermore, notwithstanding Emmett and James's attempts to situate Robin Hood in a different time period, the idea that Robin Hood lived during the time of Richard I had become the standard narrative trope. While *The Black Arrow* is not part of the Robin Hood canon of stories, it does deserve a place, if not within, then alongside the corpus of other Robin Hood texts from the nineteenth century.

Robin Hood also served as a model for late-Victorian authors writing other stories about medieval outlaws and rebels. Wat Tyler and Jack Straw, two of the leaders of the Peasants' Revolt of 1381, are often portrayed as forest outlaws who are attired in Lincoln green. William Harrison Ainsworth's *Merry England; or, Nobles and Serfs* (1874), in which Straw is a revolutionary outlaw who conspires with Tyler to foment discontent among the peasantry. Ainsworth was an admirer of Scott and earlier in his career authored two highwaymen novels entitled *Rookwood* (1834) and *Jack Sheppard* (1839). The former featured as its main protagonist the robber, Dick Turpin, transforming him from the pock-marked thug that he was in real life into a gentlemanly and handsome robber, which is the image that most British people have of Turpin today. Similarly, in the anonymously authored penny dreadful *The Sword of Freedom; or, The Boyhood Days of Jack Straw* (c. 1860), young Jack Straw is an outlaw who is loyal to the king in spite of being a robber. And as to why a Royalist outlaw would then go on to lead a revolt, the author explains this away by saying that the historical Jack Straw was probably just someone who assumed the 'real' (fictional) Straw's name.

Robin Hood rarely appeared in high art paintings. Daniel Maclise finished his *Robin Hood and His Merry Men Entertaining Richard the Lionheart in Sherwood Forest* in 1839. It is based upon a scene from *Ivanhoe*, towards the end of the book, in which the outlaws share a feast with Richard I. It is a 'merry England' depiction of the Middle Ages in which everyone is happy and has enough food to eat because all of the classes have come together. It is surprising that Robin Hood was never a popular subject for the Pre-Raphaelites. As their name suggests, this loosely connected group of artists were inspired by the art of the medieval period and rejected the realism of Renaissance art. They called themselves Pre-Raphaelites because they drew inspiration from the time before Raffaello Sanzio da Urbino (1483–1520), known nowadays simply as Raphael. The founding members of the Pre-Raphaelite Brotherhood were Dante Gabriel Rossetti (1828–82), John Everett Millais (1829–96), and William Holman Hunt (1827–1910). They were later joined in their endeavours by William Michael Rossetti (1819–1919), James Collinson (1825–81), Frederic George Stephens (1827–1907) and Thomas Woolner (1825–92). They did not always paint medieval scenes, admittedly, and many of these artists' paintings often depict classical or biblical events.

A group who were influenced by the artistic style of the Pre-Raphaelites was the Liverpool School of Painters. And from this school was William Windus (1822–1907) who painted *The Outlaw* in 1861. Windus was born into a middle-class household in Liverpool and became interested in art when a portrait painter came to paint his father. The artist subsequently took young Windus under his wing and helped to nurture what he saw as a budding talent. A trip to London in 1850 was 28-year-old Windus's first encounter with Pre-Raphaelite art, and he subsequently desired to emulate them. A few years later, in 1856, he had his first painting exhibited at the Royal Academy. The scene in *The Outlaw* is a medieval greenwood but this is not the joyful picture of merry England that audiences might expect from an outlaw tale. The figure of a woman cradles the head of an injured man. The woman turns her head slightly to the side, and appears to look apprehensive. It is as though the outlaw and the lady are being chased by the authorities. This is signified by the fact that a bloodhound is running down the hill after them. The main feature of the painting is the landscape, and the two human figures are almost slipping out of the picture at the bottom. In the Robin Hood tradition, outlaws are always associated with the natural world. The natural world represents freedom from the laws of men and freedom from mainstream society. Yet here, the unjust world of men has begun to encroach upon the outlaw world. While the title of the painting does not explicitly state that the two figures are supposed to be Robin Hood and Maid Marian, it would have been difficult for Victorian viewers not to associate the painting with the Robin Hood legend. After all, in popular culture at this time, there was no other forest dwelling outlaw who had a woman by his side.

Only Pierce Egan's *Robin Hood* reached the same levels of popularity as Scott's *Ivanhoe* had done in 1819. Scott's novel in particular functioned as the key text for subsequent Robin Hood stories. However, the novel would cease to be the primary means of the Robin Hood legend's dissemination in the succeeding century. A certain invention, which appeared at the end of the nineteenth century, would allow audiences to see and hear Robin Hood and his merry men speak, and perform great, spectacular deeds in front of their very eyes. The new medium for the dissemination of Robin Hood tales, of course, was motion picture. Robin Hood had been a hero who was known primarily by word of mouth in the medieval period, and then through text in the eighteenth and nineteenth centuries. He was about to become a visual hero.

Chapter 7

The Twentieth Century

Robin! Robin! Robin! All his merry thieves
Answer as the bugle-note shivers through the leaves:
Calling as he used to call, faint and far away,
In Sherwood, in Sherwood, about the break of day.

Alfred Noyes, *Sherwood* (1911)

Stately castles whose turrets pierced the sky have left imperishable record. – Though the storms of centuries have laid waste the works of men their spirit soars on and poets make live again the days of chivalry ... chronicles tell of warriors and statesmen, of royal Crusaders, of jousting knights. Her ballads sing of jolly friars, of troubadours, of gallant outlaws who roamed her mighty forests.

Robin Hood (1922)

'It's injustice I hate, not the Normans.'

Errol Flynn, *The Adventures of Robin Hood* (1938)

For a majority of the legend's history, Robin Hood was an adults' hero. There is no suggestion that the *Gest* was a children's rhyme; Munday's *Huntingdon* plays were produced for an adult audience; the same holds true for Walter Scott's *Ivanhoe* and Pierce Egan the Younger's *Robin Hood and Little John*. In late-Victorian literature, however, Robin Hood, and thieves and outlaws more generally, were gradually confined to the realm of children's literature. Yet there are many Robin Hoods, and what we see in the twentieth century is Robin Hood remaining a hero for adults in an entirely new medium: the motion picture. Robin Hood's fame had filtered into mainstream popular culture in United States through the publication of Howard Pyle's *The Merry Adventures of Robin Hood* in 1883, and he would have been known to the inhabitants of the dominions and colonies of the British Empire since the early nineteenth century. Edward Ives, in his *Voyage from England to India* (1773), for example, remarked that the people of Madagascar, 'pride themselves, it seems, in English names, which are bestowed upon them at the discretion or caprice of the sailors; and thus a venerable minister of state, who should have been called Sir Robert Walpole, or Cardinal Fleury, acquired the name of Robin Hood'. Robin Hood would soon become a truly international hero in the twentieth century, however, thanks to Hollywood.

Since the development of photography earlier in the nineteenth century, many inventors attempted to capture moving images by having a 'film' passing through a camera. The type of film devised varied, with some cameras capturing moving images on paper. These early motion pictures were often brief, in some cases lasting no more than a few seconds. Two motion pictures filmed in Leeds, England, by Louis Le Prince on paper strips in October 1888 are only three seconds in length, and are considered to be the first films ever produced. The most successful film technology developed for enabling early filmmakers to capture moving images, however, was celluloid. The brief films produced in the late 1880s and early 1890s were private affairs and viewed only by a select few. The first commercial screening of films was held by Le Prince and his colleagues in Paris on 28 December 1895. A lot of folklore surrounds the screening of early films. There are some reports that the Lumiere brothers' *Train Arriving at a Station* (1895) caused some spectators to panic and flee out of fear that a train was really coming towards them. Such stories that constitute 'the founding myth of early cinema' are likely to have been exaggerated because people in the 1800s were not that stupid. A lot of the evidence for episodes such as this is anecdotal or is found in the pages of satirical pieces, and even some filmmakers were prone to sensationalising the adverts of their films to attract more viewers. The practice of charging people to watch motion pictures spread throughout the Western World. Mitchell and Kenyon in the north of England produced a series of films depicting modern street life in the early 1900s and then charged a small fee for people to see them. Films became so popular because to contemporary audiences they appeared to combine science with magic and illusion; here was a technology that could capture real life as it was, so to speak.

Eventually, these short films began to tell stories instead of depicting brief moments in everyday life. Robin Hood stories have been performed many times throughout history, be it in oral recitations of medieval poems, on the stage, or sung in ballads. Reading was in fact, for a large part of the eighteenth and nineteenth centuries, often a social activity in which many middle-class families would read together for an evening's entertainment, so novels would often be performed. Robin Hood had been incorporated into every artistic and literary medium that had gone before and he would soon conquer the moving picture as well. Robin Hood's first appearance on the silver screen was in Percy Stow's *Robin Hood and His Merry Men* (1908). This film is now lost but it would have been interesting to see how Stow approached his project and upon what sources he based his portrayal of the legend. Another silent film followed shortly afterward, simply titled *Robin Hood* (1912), which in the first half is focused upon Maid Marian. There are some of the usual skirmishes with the sheriff's men; the 1908 and 1912 films were American productions, but the British and Colonial Films Company did produce *Robin Hood Outlawed* (1912) as well. Most of these were short and simple stories. *Robin Hood Outlawed* is a story of Robin rescuing Maid Marian from being kidnapped by an evil knight. These films very much resemble the plays that were staged in the eighteenth and early nineteenth centuries which told short episodes in the life of Robin Hood.

A big-budget Robin Hood picture was released in 1922 and featured Douglas Fairbanks, 'the first king of Hollywood', in the role of the outlaw. Its $1.4 million budget, a million of which was stumped up by Fairbanks himself by the company he owned, rendered it the most expensive Hollywood film up to that point and meant that the film was visually impressive. Fairbanks wanted to create a spectacle: 'Robin Hood should be made lavishly or not at all', he remarked to his brother, John. Fairbanks also aimed to make the 1190s look as accurate as possible, so his company, United Artists, hired historians to do research for the film (UA was founded by a small team of famous actors and directors which included Charlie Chaplin, D. W. Griffith, Mary Pickford, and of course Fairbanks). The first thing audiences see is the exterior of a large reconstructed castle specially built for the production. Although building a replica castle specially for a production seems like a big undertaking, in the days before transatlantic flights, it was easier and more likely cheaper to do this rather than ferry a number of actors and thousands of extras on a steamship across the sea, rent accommodation for them, and film in older, historic castles which, in all likelihood, would be unsuitable to the demands of filming anyway. Whoever the historical advisors for the movie were, it seems that both they and the screenwriters were heavily influenced by Walter Scott. In truth, many famous medievalist and fantasy writers from the twentieth century have been to some degree influenced by Scott, such as J. R. R. Tolkien and, more recently, G. R. R. Martin. The beginning of the movie is, therefore, reminiscent of *Ivanhoe*, beginning with a jousting tournament, after which the Queen of Love and Beauty, who here is Maid Marian instead of Rowena, must crown the victor. One of the contenders in the tournament is Guy of Gisborne, John's champion, and the other is Robin Hood, the 'favourite' of King Richard. Robin wins the tournament and is crowned by Marian. A feast is then held on the evening and Guy and John are plotting to usurp the throne. Marian falls in love with Robin at the feast after he intervenes when a drunken Guy is harassing her. There is a pained parting the next day as Robin Hood sets off to the Holy Land to fight alongside Richard in the crusades, which is described in the following glowing terms on the screen card: 'and so the flower of English knighthood marched on to its high purpose'. While in the Holy Land, Robin receives word from Marian that John has usurped the throne and is oppressing the people unjustly. Robin decides to return to England and once he does he is outlawed. Along with the merry men of the forest, he is a thorn in John's side. At the end, however, King Richard returns and pardons Robin and allows Marian to wed him.

Only the most dedicated Robin Hood fan or silent movie buff would today dig out Robin Hood films from the pre-talkie era. With the advent of talking pictures, however, Robin Hood became much more exciting. The greenwood was also soon realised in full colour! One film from the 1930s, however, would become a classic and, for better or for worse, give audiences an iconic image of Robin Hood which would be recognisable the world over. This film, of course, is *The Adventures of Robin Hood* (1938), starring Errol Flynn in the title role. It was phenomenally popular in the USA and in the UK upon its first release. Its reported earnings of $3,981,000 worldwide were the highest of 1930s. In an age where films might run for a maximum of six months, some members of the public record having gone to see the movie twice. The movie was visually stunning: the sets were large and hundreds of extras were involved; all of the lead players are decked out in fine and very colourful costumes. Indeed, one wonders how the outlaws in this film manage to evade detection from Gisborne and his men for the entire hour and forty minutes, given their conspicuous costumes and very visible hideouts in the forest. Although the outlaws' hideaway in the Flynn movie is nowhere near as ridiculous as the town constructed entirely from treehouses that we see in the 1990s Kevin Costner movie. In *The Adventures of Robin Hood*, might also say that the merry men are in fact too merry; hearty laughter and jokes abound and there is never a sense that Robin is in any real danger. After all, the knights and men-at-arms in this film are rather inept, in contrast to Flynn's Robin Hood who is a swashbuckling Anglo-Saxon hero, and both a master bowman and a master swordsman. It is Robin who foils the dastardly plot of Prince to John to seize the throne of England from King Richard I, who has been captured by Duke Leopold of Austria. The filmmakers here were drawing upon an actual historical event. Richard was imprisoned by Leopold at Dürnstein Castle but this was contrary to international law and so the pope punished Leopold with excommunication for having imprisoned another sovereign. Richard was then handed over to Henry VI, who styled himself 'The Holy Roman Emperor'. The Holy Roman Empire in the 1190s covered a large part of Germany, Northern Italy, Austria, and some parts of what is now Poland. It was the emperor who demanded a ransom of 150,000 marks (the approximate equivalent of £100,000). In the film, John needs money to buy the support of the Norman barons and so, upon the pretext of raising money to pay the king's ransom, he exacts monstrous poll taxes from the Saxons, all the while the Normans live in luxury. John also wishes Marian, the king's ward, to wed his lieutenant, Sir Guy of Gisborne. Marian falls in love with Robin after an ambush, however, and learns of how kind Robin is to the poor and declares in front of Prince John and Guy at the end that she is ashamed to be a part of the Norman race. In the meantime, King Richard returns to England in disguise and encounters Robin Hood in the forest; John has also learnt of Richard's return so he arranges to hastily have himself proclaimed as king by the Bishop in Nottingham. Robin and his men, along with Richard, save the day and thwart John's plans however, and Robin is pardoned, married on the spot to Maid Marian, and King Richard promises that Saxons shall thenceforth be treated kindly.

The film is not overtly political. The emphasis, as with the 1922 movie, was upon providing an enjoyable spectacle for audiences. The outlaws' code that Robin Hood makes his men swear to at the beginning of the film is a rehash of much that had been seen before in the various moral codes that Robin and his men are said to have lived by in early texts such as the *Gest* and later ones such *Ivanhoe*, and of course the late Victorian children's books. Robin's on-screen vows to take care of the downtrodden, to feed them, and provide for the sick and needy 'free men of the forest' took on a new significance in Depression-era America, however, in the context of President Roosevelt's implementation of his New Deal. In *Ivanhoe*, Robin Hood criticises King Richard I for going gallivanting abroad fighting foreign wars while his subjects in England suffer. The same criticisms of Richard are present in *The Adventures of Robin Hood*, but, much like the appropriation of the outlaws' code, would have taken on a new significance for American viewers in 1938. The rise of Hitler in Germany was bringing Europe to the brink of war but senior American politicians advocated against any intervention by America in European affairs. Senators such as Gerald P. Nye, one of the most prominent isolationists of the 1930s, reasoned that what was going on in Europe was Europe's problem. The Neutrality Act had already been passed by Congress in 1935, which prohibited any American business from exporting arms, ammunition, or any other kind of war material to nations at war. Even when war in Europe did finally break out in 1939, America initially maintained an outward neutrality. It was only in October 1941 that the American government began to reconsider their neutral stance through the Lend-Lease system. Previously, the United States would allow powers such as Britain to purchase matériel from them but only if payment was received upfront. As its name implied, Lend-Lease extended much-needed credit to a desperate United Kingdom. Of course, American neutrality laws became largely meaningless after the Japanese attack on Pearl Harbour and America's entry into the war.

In an era in which there was no home video or DVD ownership, it would be a mistake to assume that the arrival of films signalled the immediate death of Robin Hood in the publishing industry, even if books about him are rarely read today. The story of Flynn's *The Adventures of Robin Hood* was retold through the medium of print through one of the many 'annuals' that were published for children. Many of these annuals retold selected scenes from the film. Marjorie Williams published a short 'free adaptation' of the scene in which Robin Hood arrives at Nottingham Castle carrying a slain deer over his shoulders for *The Picturegoer*'s Christmas issue. We have more evidence of which Robin Hood books children were reading from Mass Observation records. It was a project started by philanthropists and filmmakers, Humphrey Jennings, Tom Harrisson, and Charles Madge, in 1937. Their aim was a simple: it was to create a record of everyday life in Britain by having volunteers write about what they had done on a given day and submit it to the archive. The first major project was to chronicle people's thoughts about the abdication of Edward VIII and the coronation of George VI in 1938. The project continued throughout the Second World War (1939–45) and was even, on occasion, used by the wartime coalition government as a means of collecting information on public morale.

Sarah Hawks Sterling's *Robin Hood and His Merry Men* (1928) was one of the most popular books requested by children at Fulham Library. This novel traces Robin Hood's life from his birth to his death, and begins by recounting a story similar to the one found in Anna Gordon's ballad, *The Birth of Robin Hood*. Robin's mother dies in childbirth and he is raised by his grandfather, Earl Richard. When Robin is 13 years old, his grandfather also dies and he is placed under the guardianship of Lord Fitzwalter, Maid Marian's father. From then on, the story just recounts the well-known ballads. The popularity of Sterling's novel is surprising because it is usually thought Pyle's *The Merry Adventures of Robin Hood* had effectively cornered the market for Robin Hood books in the twentieth century. When Penguin Books decided to publish a Robin Hood story as part of their Classics range in 1938, it was Pyle's story that they chose for the collection, rather than any English author. Sterling's novel is written in the same spirit as the late Victorian children's Robin Hood books: it is very conservative and rehearses many of the storylines from Scott's *Ivanhoe*. In Mass Observation records, we also see the continuing popularity of Scott's *Ivanhoe* among children in London, in particular the Penguin Books 6d edition. The same record also records that nineteenth-century school editions of *Ivanhoe* remain in circulation and are popular among youths. We see another unnamed child opting for Sterling's book in 1942. In Marylebone, a Mass Observation worker saw a child carrying four books on their way home: Sterling's *Robin Hood*, and some anonymous works *The War of the Wireless*, *Shadow of the Swastika*, and *The First Quarter*. The child had chosen Sterling's *Robin Hood* because it had been recommended by a friend and they even told the interviewer that it generally took them half a week to read through a full book.

Mass Observation did not focus merely upon children, however, for the investigators also interviewed adults. What is interesting are the records of some of the Variety shows which were held on evenings. On 14 November 1942, a show was held in Bournemouth to raise money for civilians in USSR (the Soviet Union was part of the Allied Forces at this point). The theme of the show was 'Merrie England' and three Robin Hood songs were sung at the event. None of these songs were of the traditional ballad type, however, as they were taken from MacNally's eighteenth-century play as well as Macfarren's Victorian opera. This might at first seem strange that variety show organisers would choose dated Victorian operatic songs instead of traditional ballads. There are likely to be two reasons for this. The first is that in the twentieth century, when early modern Robin Hood ballads were being published, they were usually done so without the melodies supplied. Reprints of Ritson's *Robin Hood* had ceased including the musical scores to the ballads with the second 1820 edition. Edward W. Fithian's *The Life of Robin Hood* (c. 1900), which, like Ritson's book, included a biography of Robin Hood as well as the text of numerous Robin Hood songs, did not include any of the melodies to the songs, and neither did Arthur Quiller Couch's *The Oxford Book of Ballads* (1911). It was also rare to find anybody who still sang Robin Hood ballads in the twentieth century, with the exception of dedicated folk music performers. Even when performers of traditional songs did perform Robin Hood songs, it was often a very niche market to which they were catering. The broadside trade had also virtually disappeared by the Edwardian period (except in Scotland, whose broadside and chapbook trade lasted into the twentieth century). The invention of the radio could likewise transmit new music direct into people's homes. However, the sale of sheet music of airs and songs from famous operas, for both private use and performance in local pageants and events, was common practice among publishers in both Britain and America. The years between c. 1890 and c. 1940 are in fact called 'the golden age of sheet music' among some pop music historians. A further factor to consider in discussing the reuse of Macfarren's song in a 1940s variety show is that this particular one was held in 1942, at the height of the war. There is little that is patriotic in early modern Robin Hood ballads, apart from one exception entitled *The Noble Fisherman*, in which, bizarrely, Robin Hood travels to Whitby, becomes a fisherman, and fights off a French ship. Victorian songs celebrating Englishness were obviously a better choice for a wartime variety show than dated early modern ballads, many of which actually depict the great English hero getting a beating from various figures.

In 1956, the last 'Victorian' Robin Hood children's book was written by Roger Lancelyn Green, entitled *The Adventures of Robin Hood*. The word 'Victorian' is used here to mean a set of values rather than a time period, because Green's work is similar in many ways to the books that were written in the late nineteenth century, with moderately conservative political outlook. Green's interest in all things medieval began early in life when he was a student at Merton College, Oxford, where he studied under the famous children's novelist, C. S. Lewis (1898–1963). He remained friends with his tutor in later life and apparently it was Green who suggested to Lewis that he name his popular children's books *The Chronicles of Narnia*, when Lewis began writing them in the 1950s. Along with Lewis, at university, Green was a member of the Inklings reading group, a society of medievalist and fantasy fiction enthusiasts who counted among their ranks J. R. R. Tolkien, author of *The Lord of the Rings* (1892–1973). Just like many of the authors that had gone before him, Green had based his work upon reading Munday's *Huntingdon* plays, the ballads from Ritson's *Robin Hood*, Scott's *Ivanhoe*, and Peacock's *Maid Marian*. In keeping with Scott's *Ivanhoe*, which for many children's books appears to be just as, if not more, important than earlier ballad material, Robin Hood is an Anglo-Saxon outlaw. And neither does Green's book innovate upon the now tired formula of Victorian Robin Hood books; all that he does, as many before him did, is simply retell the ballad stories in prose. Green probably read Munday's Huntingdon plays at some point as well, for Prince John has a sycophantic sidekick named Worman. Unlike his tutor, Lewis, and his friend, Tolkien, however, Green's Robin Hood, as well as his other medievalist stories such as *King Arthur*, failed to make him famous, although he did make a comfortable living from his other literary works overall.

Shortly before Lancelyn Green's book was published, however, the Victorian upper middle-class Robin Hood was realised on the small screen in *The Adventures of Robin Hood* (1955–59), which was originally broadcast on ITV in the United Kingdom, and then on CBS in the United States. Robin Hood, played by Richard Greene, was not the daredevil action hero seen in Flynn's *Adventures of Robin Hood* but a more reserved hero. Stephen Knight calls Green's Robin Hood 'everyone's favourite uncle', and argues he represents the paternalist ideals of the 1950s British welfare state. There is some incorporation of earlier ballad stories into this series, as well as many new adventures, although many of them were forgettable. While at first glance the series was fairly apolitical, Hannah Weinstein, the show's producer, had hired a number of writers who had been blacklisted in the United States to write episodes for the series. These writers, such as Ring Lardner Jr, Waldo Salt, and Robert Lees had been forbidden by Hollywood from writing for studios because of their hard left political views; in the words of the Motion Picture Association of America, 'we will not knowingly employ a Communist or a member of any party or group which advocates the overthrow of the government of the United States'. The reason for this heavy-handed approach towards writers with anti-capitalist beliefs was because this was the era of McCarthyism, during which the American establishment, led by Senator Joseph McCarthy, grew increasingly paranoid that some American citizens were participating in 'Un-American Activities'. The House of Representatives Un-American Activities Committee (HUAC) was actually established in 1939 to investigate private citizens who were suspected of holding communist sympathies, but the department's activities grew more fervent during the Cold War. Thus, while the content of the show was uncontroversial and even bland, its production was actually a subversive act which defied the American authorities.

The 1970s witnessed three major new portrayals of Robin Hood on the small and big screen. The first Robin Hood movie of the decade was Disney's animated *Robin Hood* (1973). Disney had released a live-action film entitled *The Story of Robin Hood* back in 1952, which enjoyed some moderate success at the box office and received favourable reviews, especially for Richard Todd's performance in the title role. The film has been easily forgotten, however, the Disney Corporation's most memorable portrayal of Robin Hood came in their feature-length cartoon. This film is a story of Robin Hood and the 'merry menagerie', to quote the movie poster's tagline, for all of the characters are anthropomorphic creatures. Robin Hood and Maid Marian are portrayed as a fox and a vixen respectively. Together with Little John (a bear), Allen-a-Dale (a cockerel), and Friar Tuck (a badger). The villains of the story were not cute and cuddly like the outlaws, however, but were more depicted as more dangerous animals: Prince John (a lion), Sir Hiss (a snake, and a character who was based upon Guy of Gisborne), and the Sheriff of Nottingham (a wolf). Stephen Knight has suggested that the film on one level reflects the deep racialism embedded in contemporary American society because the good animals were cute and cuddly creatures, and were often depictions of animals from the Anglo-American world. The bad animals, in contrast, were from Africa and Asia. Such an argument might work for a character such as Sir Hiss, but there is little evidence to suggest that a lion reflects racialism. Even if it was intended as such, it is doubtful that viewers in Britain would have interpreted the film in that way. A lion after all is one of England's national symbols, and are generally viewed as majestic creatures. It is also doubtful that children, who were the primary audience for such a film, were aware of the supposed racialism behind the depictions of the merry men.

As is the case with many novels, very few film or television series tell the outlaw's story from his birth to death. Most Robin Hood stories from the nineteenth century onwards end with King Richard returning from the Crusades and pardoning Robin. The series entitled *The Legend of Robin Hood* (1975) is different in this respect. Episode one bears some resemblance to the beginning of Pierce Egan's novel, in which Robin is delivered as a baby to the house of a forester to be cared for; secrecy surrounds his birth and young Robin, as in Egan's novel, grows up in ignorance of the fact that he is the heir to the Earldom of Huntingdon. Eventually he is outlawed and the usual adventures of thwarting the plans of Prince John and Guy of Gisborne follow. At the end, after having been restored to his true inheritance and returning to his ancestral home, he develops a fever. He dispatches a servant to fetch some berries from the wood, but the man is intercepted by a nun. As Robin lays on sick bed he opens his eyes and finds the nun standing over him. She feeds him a goblet purportedly containing a herbal remedy but which actually contains poison; as Robin lays dying, she informs him that Guy of Gisborne was her brother and she is taking revenge upon Robin for his death.

The year following the broadcast of *The Legend of Robin Hood* saw two big name movie stars enter the greenwood, Sean Connery and Audrey Hepburn, who played Robin Hood and Maid Marian respectively in Richard Lester's *Robin and Marian*. This film gave audiences the story of 'Robin Hood's Death', which was its working title until quite late in the production process when the producers decided that it would be more marketable with the former. An aged Robin returns from the crusade, having been conscripted by the king as a punishment for his having been an outlaw. When he returns, Robin finds that Marian has become a nun. The two initially quarrel and then Robin finds out that his old enemy, the Sheriff of Nottingham, is still treating Saxons cruelly, so he reluctantly takes up the cause of social justice once again. After he is wounded towards the end of the film, he goes to Marian's private chamber to rest. In a twist upon the original ballad story, it is there that Marian decides to kill him and herself. When Robin wakes up she informs him of what she has done and, oddly, he accepts his fate with barely a murmur. Thus ends the hero's life with little fanfare.

Reviews for Robin and Marian were mixed. Most reviewers praised Connery and Hepburn for their acting; the plot, however, was another matter indeed; Roger Ebert complained that the film could not decide what type of film it wanted to be. The humorous moments, for Ebert, were incongruous with the film's pretensions to tragedy. Another factor which perhaps influenced the film's mixed reception is the fact that medieval historical dramas had become a subject for humour with not only Disney's *Robin Hood* but also the release of *Monty Python and the Holy Grail* (1975). For a brief time in the 1970s, the medieval period was either a cartoon world, or it was peopled by nymphomaniac nuns, knights who say 'ni', and Sir Robin the

Not-Quite-So-Brave-as-Sir-Lancelot. Ebert noted the lack of comedy in *Robin and Marian* and found it a little odd, saying that the character of Robin Hood ideally should be an ageless adolescent who plays merry pranks.

There was another Robin Hood movie that did not fare well with either critics or audiences. This was *Wolfshead: The Legend of Robin Hood* (1973), which is essentially *Ivanhoe* in all but name. David Warbeck plays Robin of Locksley, who is a simple yeoman just like in *Ivanhoe*, and who is also accompanied by a Gyrth who is a swineherd, much like Gurth in Scott's novel. Although the film release was intended to kickstart a franchise, it was ultimately unsuccessful. In the world of Robin Hood in 1973, it was evidently a battle between the fox and the wolf, and the fox won.

While there have been many films dedicated to telling only the story of Robin Hood, the popularity of movie adaptations of Scott's *Ivanhoe* does deserve attention. The fact that the novel contained three spectacular scenes – the jousting tournament, the Siege of Torquilstone, and Ivanhoe's final fight with Front-de-Boeuf – it was perfect for to adapt for early cinema. Two adaptations of *Ivanhoe* appeared in 1913, a British version and a French version. The first big-budget film version of Scott's novel was released in 1952, and starred Robert Taylor in the title role, and Elizabeth Taylor as Ivanhoe's love interest, Rowena, and Harold Wartender as Robin of Locksley. The film significantly departs from Scott's source material, with Ivanhoe taking a more active role in the battles against Prince John's Templars, with the help of Robin Hood. The film is also noteworthy for its very sympathetic portrayal of Scott's Jewish character, Isaac of York. Scott himself, way back in 1819, used the character of Isaac and his daughter, Rebecca, to argue the case for religious toleration. But the 1952 movie would have had significant resonance for viewers who had just lived through the Second World War, after which news of the Holocaust would have been fresh in people's minds. While King Richard plays a prominent role in the novel, in this version of *Ivanhoe* he has a minor role in this movie and becomes, as he is in so many other Robin Hood movie adaptations, 'King Richard of the Last Reel'.

Conventional wisdom rules that bad books make good movies and television shows. John Galsworthy's terrible *Forsyte Saga* books were great source material for an early soap opera. Being a literary masterpiece, *Ivanhoe* in general is only well-suited to film and television when it has talented actors and skilled writers to realise its ambition. Having a big budget also helps somewhat in this respect, although it is possible for a television series of *Ivanhoe* to be made on the cheap, yet still respect the source material and be rather good. The version of it that adheres most closely to Scott's novel is *Ivanhoe* (1982). It featured some actors who were, or would go on to become, big names in the movie world. The fresh-faced Anthony Andrews was cast in the role of Ivanhoe, riding on the success of his role alongside Jeremy Irons in *Brideshead Revisited* (1981). The future star of *Jurassic Park* (1993), Sam Neil, played Brian de Bois-Guilbert. Robin Hood, however, is a minor role in this version of *Ivanhoe*, reduced to being simply an amiable non-entity by the scriptwriters who place too much emphasis on the part of Richard I's actions in the novel.

The Anthony Andrews version of *Ivanhoe* preceded by two years one of the best portrayals of Robin Hood: *Robin of Sherwood*, a television series that was broadcast between 1984 and 1986. The producer and writer of this series, Paul Knight and Richard Carpenter respectively, had made another successful outlaw TV series a few years before entitled *Dick Turpin* (1978–81). The series was fairly successful in commercial terms and depicted the famous eighteenth-century highwayman as a moderately anti-establishment figure who cannily outwits the rich and the powerful. Knight and Carpenter then revisited this formula, and with much greater success, in *Robin of Sherwood*. Robin of Locksley, played by Michael Praed, is a good-looking but tough yeoman who is adopted by a forest spirit named Herne the Hunter to become the hero of the downtrodden people of Nottingham. When the yeoman Robin of Locksley dies after a final heroic battle against the sheriff, Herne adopts another man named Robin, who is Robert, Earl of Huntingdon, played by Jason Connery, to be the people's hero.

Robin of Sherwood was filmed during the height of Thatcherism in the United Kingdom: the prime minister, Margaret Thatcher, had been victorious in the Falklands War (1982), and had faced down a national strike by the miners' unions in 1984; her government then began to privatise a number of previously state-owned industries in an attempt to 'Roll Back the State' and curb what she saw as the negative economic effects of socialism. Thatcher was a disciple of the Austrian economist Frederick Hayek and rejected the 'consensus' model of government (the consensus model stressed cooperation between government, managers, and unions in industrial relations and the government committed itself to providing full employment for everyone). Thatcher's market reforms signalled the abolition of this and she wanted to transform Britain into a country whose economy was governed by the principles of free market capitalism and consumerism. Cultural portrayals of outlaws, ever since the days of *A Gest of Robyn Hode*, have always been an attempt on the part of their writers to glorify 'the old ways'; in the *Gest*, Robin and his men live according to older social customs, governing their actions in a quasi-chivalrous manner and owing loyalty to one another in the face of greed engendered by the breakdown of feudalism in the fifteenth century and the onset of capitalism. So *Robin of Sherwood* represented the breakdown of the more paternalist Keynesian economics that were adopted by both Labour and Conservative governments after the Second World War. Thus we see Robin of Locksley as the paternalist outlaw who provides for those in need, and the Sheriff of Nottingham, excellently played by Nickolas Grace, as a money-obsessed individualist with few moral scruples.

While the late 1970s and 1980s witnessed far-reaching economic reforms, it was also a period which saw the emergence of 'new age' spirituality. This is an ideology which holds that humans can only receive Enlightenment through reconnecting with the natural world, after which they will become reacquainted with 'god' once again (the concept of God is vague in new age philosophy, which is accepting of all religions but rejects the 'narrow-mindedness' of organised religion). Robin Hood, who lives in the forest and is effectively at one with the natural world, and, so it was theorised by some fringe researchers, was actually a composite spirit of a forest elf, was in many respects a perfect new age figure. Thus, in addition to 'typical' Robin Hood episodes which see him thwarting the sheriff's plans and meeting strangers in the forest, *Robin of Sherwood* also introduces a number of new plot elements into the Robin Hood legend. There is the notable inclusion of Herne the Hunter, a forest god who chooses Robin of Locksley to serve as a symbol of hope and resistance against the sheriff and unjust authority. Although the series portrays Herne as an ancient, mythical, pre-Christian being, the reality is that he is actually a Shakespearean invention and first appeared in *The Merry Wives of Windsor* (1597). He also was originally a figure associated solely with Windsor Forest; William Harrison Ainsworth did feature him in his novel *Windsor Castle* (1842), where he is portrayed as a ghost who haunts the local forest and interacts with both Henry VIII and Anne Boleyn. In spite of the fact that there is no conclusive evidence to suggest that Herne was anything other than an invention of Shakespeare, however, many Wiccans mistakenly adhere to the belief that Herne is indeed a timeless god who, some Wiccans argue, goes all the way back to the druids.

As well as the inclusion of Herne the Hunter, *Robin of Sherwood* includes a number of mystical and supernatural elements. This stemmed from a desire on Carpenter's part to portray the medieval past 'as it was', however, rather than being a spiritual philosophy that he personally held. As

Carpenter once said in an interview that, 'the Middle Ages were extremely superstitious and much remained of the old pre-Christian fertility and tree worship religions ... Vestiges of this still remain throughout Europe.' The first episode of series one, for instance, sees Robin having to rescue Marian from the clutches of Baron Simon de Belleme, who intends to sacrifice Marian to Satan and is able to hypnotise his bodyguards into fighting for him. A rather creepy episode entitled *Cromm Cruac*, which sees the outlaws venturing into an unknown village on the edge of the forest, where there is food and drink aplenty, but no children to be seen. The inhabitants, who are over a century old but appear youthful, worship a pre-Christian Irish god named Cromm Cruach who demanded the sacrifice of the villagers' children in return for plentiful harvests. The series in fact ends with Robert of Huntingdon facing one of his archenemies, a warlock with supernatural powers named Gulnar, played by Richard O'Brien. The series' new age credentials were cemented by the fact that the entire soundtrack was provided by the new age folk-rock band, Clannad.

The late twentieth century has seen many more portrayals of Robin Hood on both the big and small screen. For many readers, *Robin Hood: Prince of Thieves* (1991) will be one of the most memorable Robin Hood movies in recent history. This was a big set-piece Hollywood movie which cared little for what had gone before in previous portrayals of Robin Hood. This approach is admittedly not always a bad thing if done correctly. After all, Scott's innovation in 1819, in making Robin an Anglo-Saxon freedom fighter loyal to the king, would correspond to most people's image of Robin Hood. *Robin Hood: Prince of Thieves*, however, descends into farce early on. Alan Rickman who plays the Sheriff of Nottingham seems to be the only one who has realised that he is not acting in a serious historical drama but is in fact performing in what is essentially a comedy. Yet there are many things wrong with the film: it must be the only portrayal of Robin Hood throughout history in which viewers find the sheriff a more likeable character than Robin himself. Indeed, this must be the only Robin Hood movie in history in which viewers actually desire to see the sheriff succeed. The geographical setting seemingly mattered little to the makers of *Robin Hood: Prince of Thieves*. After a daring escape from a god-forsaken prison in the Middle East, Robin returns home with a Saracen, Azeem, played by Morgan Freeman, and arrives at Dover. To get home to Locksley, Robin says, will only take until nightfall on foot. However, the pair of them first make a large and unnecessary detour to Hadrian's Wall. It is at the wall where Robin rescues a young boy from being killed by Guy of Gisborne.

How strange, then, for Robin to encounter this same boy in Sherwood Forest, for he is actually the son of Little John.

The story is one in which Robin returns from the crusades to find his father dead and his estate and lands in ruins. Only the blind family servant has survived to inform Robin of what has happened: the Sheriff of Nottingham and his supporters, who at the beginning of the movie are dressed in costumes resembling the Ku Klux Klan, killed his father because he would not join them in helping the sheriff to seize control of the kingdom in Richard's absence. Having already been in a dispute with Guy of Gisborne up at Hadrian's Wall, Robin has no choice but to become an outlaw with his fellow traveller, Azeem. So Robin ventures into Sherwood Forest where he meets the usual entourage of outlaws, and volunteers to lead them, while of course fighting for his own cause, which is the restitution of his lands. Yet Robin actually appears to despise the peasants of Nottingham when they come to him for help; the sheriff, in revenge for the outlaws' depredations, destroys a village and naturally the villagers challenge Robin about his actions; in reply he merely chastises them for not being strong enough to fight back and reminds them that the sheriff would be just as cruel to them if Robin was not in England. Meantime, it turns out that Marian is actually the cousin of King Richard, so the sheriff vows to woo her in order to cement his claim to the throne, but of course he is thwarted in both his attempts to raise money by Robin Hood who steals from the rich to give to the poor. A showdown occurs at Nottingham Castle between the sheriff's men and the outlaws (it seems that the Sheriff has managed to somehow hire Celts as mercenaries even though Celts did not exist by the 1190s). At the end, Robin and Marian are married and King Richard returns to bless the marriage.

John Aberth says that the inclusion of the Middle Eastern Azeem in the film, along with Marian's portrayal as a strong and independent woman, suggests that the filmmakers were attempting to be politically correct in their retelling of Robin Hood by pushing diversity, multiculturalism, and feminism. During the late 1980s and early 1990s, the USA pursued an assimilationist approach to immigration. However, the inclusion of Azeem is more likely to simply be the result of the fact that the producers wished to emulate *Robin of Sherwood* which had successfully included a Saracen before. Presumably, the makers of *Robin of Sherwood* had at some point seen Stocqueler's *Maid Marian* which, as we have seen, is the first time that Robin brings a Muslim character back to England with him.

The 1990s, furthermore, was the era that witnessed the emergence of so-called 'third wave feminism'. While second wave feminists during the 1960s had mainly political goals, feminists from the 1990s were more often than not concerned with critiquing established gender roles. However, Aberth's point about the film somehow pushing 'politically correct' feminism is not so stable when we consider that, although Marian is indeed depicted as a strong, feisty, and independent woman at the beginning of the movie, in which she can hold her own in a swordfight against even Robin himself, she loses any sort of independence she has and reverts to being a delicate little lady when the sheriff kidnaps her towards the end of the movie. Aberth's position does not account for the character of the witch as well, which simply regurgitates some quite dated views about witches from the nineteenth century. While *Robin Hood: Prince of Thieves* seems to be an advocate for third wave feminist ideals, then, the reality is that any freedom or equality granted to Marian in the film is contained and ultimately restricted.

When folk singers have covered Robin Hood songs, they have, admittedly, never been chart toppers. In the early 1990s, however, there was an expectation that any big blockbuster movie would be accompanied by a chart-topping song performed by a big-name singer. The world was therefore given Bryan Adams's *Everything I Do* which surprisingly remained at number one in the US charts seven weeks, and in the UK charts for sixteen weeks. The lyrics themselves make no reference to Robin Hood, but the 1980s and 1990s were the golden age of the music video. A singer's popularity often depended upon the quality of the accompanying video spectacle. Thus, the music video for *Everything I Do* featured Bryan Adams's singing in a forest with some of the exciting scenes from *Prince of Thieves* interspersed throughout. Contemporary audiences loved not only the song, evident by its chart success, but also the music video itself. The organisers of the MTV Movie Awards decided that, along with Bryan Adams's video and some of the movie tie-in songs for that year, such as Guns 'n' Roses' *You Could Be Mine* (from *Terminator 2: Judgment Day*), that a whole new category of award had to be created for this new movie-marketing medium. Thus the MTV Movie Award for Best Song from a Movie was born in 1992, and the first gong went to Adams's *Everything I Do*. The music video for Adams's song, however, likely reached a greater audience than the actual film did initially, for even if a casual MTV or VH1 viewer had not been to see the film, they would have seen scenes from *Robin Hood: Prince of Thieves* on their televisions.

Another part of the film's marketing was the release of related action figures and playsets. Parents could buy their children Sherwood Forest and

Nottingham Castle playsets, with the actual action figures sold separately. However, the action figures in effect tell their own story about gender expectations placed upon young boys in the 1990s. The action figures depict the ideal male body of the early 1990s which was muscular and well-built. This was the era of the original 'Diet Coke man', of course, in which female office workers ogle a muscular man while on their break. While the actor, Kevin Costner, was well-toned in the movie, the corresponding action figure depicts a Robin Hood who looks as though he is on steroids. The action figure of Christian Slater's Will Scarlet, who in the film is of a toned-but-slight build, is likewise beefed up.

At the same time as *Prince of Thieves* was released, a darker, grittier, and less gimmicky Robin Hood movie was released simply titled *Robin Hood* (1991), and it featured Patrick Bergin in the title role. The plot of this film bears a passing resemblance to the novel *Robin Hood: A Tale of the Olden Time* (1819). Robin is a local lord who, at the beginning of the movie, stops a Norman lord named Miles Folcanet from inflicting a brutal punishment upon a lowly Saxon poacher. Folcanet, enraged and humiliated, immediately goes to see the Sheriff of Nottingham, named Baron Daguerre. The sheriff is reluctant to inflict any punishment on Robin because he is actually good friends with him. Robin initially agrees to submit to a punishment, but when he is in the sheriff's hall about to receive a flogging, he refuses, insults the sheriff, fights off a few armed guards and takes to the forest where he adopts the name of Robin Hood. A few typical Robin Hood escapades follow; robbing travellers and being a general thorn in the side of his old friend, the sheriff. Robin also falls in love with Daguerre's niece, Maid Mariane, played by Uma Thurman, but it turns out that she is to be married to Falconet! The climax of the movie sees Robin and his men interrupt the wedding, declare his love for Mariane, and be reconciled with Daguerre. The film received some praise, notably for the quality of its actors' performances. Howard Rosenberg in *The Los Angeles Times* stated that one its best qualities was its atmosphere, having used muted colours to emphasise the 'bleakness' of the medieval period in which Robin Hood is said to have lived. Yet Rosenberg recognised that this was still just a run-of-the-mill Robin Hood story which rehearsed well-known narrative tropes found since *Ivanhoe*. The big Robin Hood blockbuster for the 1990s was clearly *Robin Hood: Prince of Thieves*.

Some of the stories of Robin Hood that have circulated throughout history have always had a comic streak in them. Walter Scott included several comic characters and scenes in *Ivanhoe*. Pierce Egan's *Robin Hood* is also amusing in parts, as are several late-Victorian penny dreadfuls. In the 1990s, however, the comic elements of Robin Hood reached an entirely new level. In order to capitalise upon the success of *Robin Hood: Prince of Thieves*, Mel Brookes released *Robin Hood: Men in Tights* (1993) starring Cary Elwes as the titular hero. The movie mocks both Flynn and Costner's Robin Hood characters, with Elwes sardonically remarking that unlike every other Robin Hood on film, he is the only one who can speak with an English accent. Although it should be noted that some linguists argue that the American accent is closer to how early modern English would have been spoken than the current English accent because it has undergone fewer changes over time. In *Men in Tights*, in place of Friar Tuck we have Rabbi Tuck; as in *Prince of Thieves*, there is also a witch who is obsessed with the Sheriff of Rottingham, who is actually in love with Marian – who wears a chastity belt. However, there is a comical love triangle which sees the witch who lives in the castle besotted with the sheriff. The idea that Robin Hood wears tights, a tradition which originally began in the Victorian era when women played Robin Hood in 'low' theatre (and thereby preserve their modesty), is satirised in the 'Manly Men' song.

Scott Allen Nollen, who has researched Robin Hood films in depth, has very few good words to say about *Men in Tights*. The film was released at a point in Mel Brookes's career when he had run out of good ideas and was relying too heavily on parodying existing franchises with slapstick comedy and sexual innuendoes. Thus, according to Nollen, *Men in Tights* is simply a medieval *Spaceballs* (1987). This criticism is justified: it is as though many of the scenes in Brookes's film are simply lifted from Errol Flynn's *The Adventures of Robin Hood* and Costner's *Robin Hood: Prince of Thieves* with lewd dialogue inserted into them. Yet *Robin Hood: Men in Tights* was not the only farcical portrayal of Robin Hood to be released during the late twentieth century. In some ways, the story of Robin Hood reaches people who would probably be otherwise uninterested in medieval history when he is incorporated into other franchises. As a popular hero in the early 1990s, the creators of *Star Trek: The Next Generation* decided to have one of the recurring characters, Q, an all-powerful intergalactic rogue and frequent antagonist of Captain Picard, send the captain and the crew of the USS Enterprise back to Sherwood Forest. Picard plays the role of Robin Hood, and his crew assume the roles of the merry men. Two of the regular *Next Generation* characters, Deanna Troi and Beverley Crusher, were denied the chance to have a sword fight because the producers did not want to be historically inaccurate. The two characters, therefore, assumed the roles of typical medieval maidens. This was in spite of the fact that the episode sees the fictional crew of a spaceship from the twenty-third century transported back to Sherwood Forest, in which, presumably, any pretensions to historical accuracy should have been meaningless. Such attitudes towards the representation of woman and other minorities are often part of wider problems regarding issues of race and gender in sci-fi and fantasy medievalism. Many people will happily watch a show or read a novel with no pretensions to historical accuracy but will then bizarrely object if women or black people are given parts that appear to be historically inaccurate.

Before Star Trek, there were some truly enjoyable, if very strange, attempts to insert Robin Hood into the world of science fiction. The first volume of Simon Hawke's twelve volume *Time Wars* book series, published between 1984 and 1991, was entitled *The Ivanhoe Gambit*. In this novel, soldiers from the future travel into the past to fight alongside famous figures from history in various wars and battles from the medieval period to the twentieth century. The first science fiction depiction of Robin Hood appeared some years before both *Star Trek* and *The Ivanhoe Gambit*, however: this was the Canadian television series *Rocket Robin Hood* (1966–69). In this show, in the thirtieth century, Robin Hood, is the captain of a space ship, and much like Captain Kirk in *Star Trek: The Original Series* (1966–69), he gets into scrapes with aliens of many varieties. A flavour of the show's content can be gained from the ballad-esque lyrics which are featured on the opening credits:

> Come gather around me. Space travellers surround me,
> Hark now to the ballad of Rocket Robin Hood.
> I may well confound you, astound you spellbound you,
> With heroes and villains, the bad and the good …
> At the sight of Robin, take your stand,
> With the gallant leader of our band.
> Send a joyous shout throughout the land,
> For Rocket Robin Hood!

This series is remembered with fondness by Canadian Robin Hood scholar, Allen Wright, who remembers watching endless re-runs on Canadian TV in his youth. This is because Canadian law stated that television stations in Canada must devote a certain amount of airtime to films and TV shows made in Canada, in part to offset American programmes from gaining too much influence. It was a way of preserving Canadian culture in the face of imports from its larger neighbour to the south. As Wright says, this meant that *Rocket Robin Hood* was never aired again after its initial run in other countries, but was re-run countless times in Canada so Canadian stations could fulfil their quota of domestically-produced shows.

If the *Star Trek* Robin Hood episode was a light-hearted romp through a fantasy medieval period which did not take itself too seriously, there were some film and television adaptations of the Robin Hood story which were intended as serious works, but which unintentionally become a complete joke. Under this banner belongs a series entitled *The New Adventures of Robin Hood*, which ran from January 1997 until December 1998. This series was produced in order to capitalise upon the success of other contemporary historical/fantasy shows such as *Hercules* (1995–97), starring Kevin Sorbo, and *Xena: The Warrior Princess* (1995–2001), starring Lucy Lawless. As in *Robin Hood: Prince of Thieves*, geography mattered little to the show's creators. Sherwood Forest is a truly international place in this series; the first episode sees Robin and his men fight against an invasion of Genghis Khan's Mongolian warriors who have somehow made their way over to Nottingham. The second episode then sees twelfth-century Robin Hood fight against a Viking invasion. The concept of historical accuracy in any period film is undeniably problematic and, as an ideal, is virtually unattainable. This is perhaps more so in any adaptation of the Robin Hood story where there is no single authoritative text or record of a historical event upon which to draw. However, audiences do, all the same, have the right to expect that filmmakers have at least picked up a history book.

While some of the 1990s Robin Hood films and TV series were often jokey and unintentionally funny, the next century would see the rise of a more serious medievalism in popular culture. The first instalment of *The Lord of the Rings* movies was released and enjoyed unprecedented commercial success in 2001. New films featuring King Arthur and a heavily historicised Robin Hood were released in 2004 and 2010 respectively, and the present time is, of course, the era of *Game of Thrones* and *Viking* mania.

Chapter 8

The Twenty-First Century

If any reader please to try,
As I direction show,
The truth of this brave history,
Hee'l find it true I know.

And I shall think my labour well,
Bestowed, to purpose good,
When't shall be sayd that I did tell
True tales of Robbin Hood.

Martin Parker,
A True Tale of Robin Hood (c. 1630)

It is clear that the medium for disseminating new and innovative Robin Hood stories is now through either the big or the small screen. Most people in the twentieth century would have encountered Robin Hood on the big screen or through their television sets. This trend has continued, and it is doubtful that Robin Hood fiction books will ever be as popular as they were in the Victorian period.

In 2001, Disney once again gave the world a new depiction of Robin Hood in *Princess of Thieves*. It is presented as a sequel to the legend of Robin Hood and featured Keira Knightly as Gwyn, who is the daughter of Robin of Huntingdon. Robin was pardoned by Richard I but, upon the king's death, his old enemy Prince John ascends the throne. With the help of the Sheriff of Nottingham, played by Malcolm MacDowell, Robin Hood is arrested. It is up to Gwyn to gather the merry men and rescue her father from the clutches of the sheriff. It was an enjoyable, if ultimately forgettable movie.

In 2006, the BBC released a television series named *Robin Hood* which ran for three seasons. This can justifiably be called 'the Boyband Robin

Hood'. The title role was played by Jonas Armstrong, and his merry men were all played by good-looking men under the age of 35, and all dressed in costumes more akin to modern hoodies and combat trousers than medieval yeoman attire. The series was influenced by the *Matrix* series of films and its 'bullet time' cinematography. The first episode sees Robin Hood returning from the crusades and stopping for refreshment at a farmer's house. After Robin makes a pass at this daughter the farmer is enraged and attacks Robin. Just as in the fight scenes in the Matrix, time is slowed down as Robin avoids the blows made towards him.

This is a Robin Hood who, in the first two series, never actually kills his opponents but merely incapacitates them. The reason for this is that he has developed an aversion to all forms of violence having fought in the crusades. In the early episodes, in fact, the BBC attempted to show a mentally traumatised Robin Hood who had 'crusader sickness', which is depicted as a medieval form of post-traumatic stress disorder. However, this theme is not developed in later episodes, and his aversion to violence is a departure from preceding Robin Hood stories; even in the most respectable Victorian Robin Hood stories, he is still a man who will take a life when necessary.

The casting is an example of the BBC's 'colour blind' policy of choosing the best actors for the role in historical dramas regardless of skin colour. The producers innovated upon the established precedent of including a Muslim character by having a woman play the role instead. There is also a black Friar Tuck, unlike the female Muslim character, Djaq, however, Tuck, played by David Harewood, is not depicted as a medieval immigrant but as a native Englishman. The BBC's multiculturalism drive of the early 2000s is evident when he claims Britain as 'my country'. There was very little opposition to the casting of a black Friar Tuck, surprisingly, and even the conservative *Daily Mail* had little to say on the subject of Harewood's skin colour in their coverage of the series. The truth of the matter is that many viewers were probably surprised at the casting choice, but very few were actually bothered by it, certainly not the young adults at whom the show was aimed. The BBC then followed their practice of colour-blind casting in their follow up television show *Merlin* (2008–12), in which Arthur's true love, Guinevere, is played by Angel Coulby.

The Jonas Armstrong series is also comical in several places. The merry men often crack jokes as they are fighting the sheriff's soldiers, reciting lines from older UK children's TV shows such as the *Chuckle Brothers*. The BBC, whenever it turns its hand to Robin Hood, seems to enjoy presenting a camper version of the story, especially if, as with the Jonas Armstrong series, it is aimed primarily at children. There was a show entitled *Maid Marian and her Merry Men* (1989–94) which was just a series of ridiculous spoofs of contemporary Robin Hood movies, as well as other unrelated movies such as *Jurassic Park*. The show did put Marian in the limelight and portrayed her as a woman who was surrounded by a buffoonish Robin Hood and stupid men. The Sheriff of Nottingham in this series likewise has in his entourage some rather inept soldiers who always fail to catch the merry men.

The BBC's penchant for comedic portrayals of Robin Hood can also be found in a recent episode of *Doctor Who* entitled *Robot of Sherwood*. The themes of some of the earlier Robin Hood ballads are present. The Doctor assumes the role of Robin Hood's challenger in a typical Robin-Hood-meets-his-match scenario. There is also an archery contest, which Robin wins by splitting the shaft of the arrow in the target. Allen-a-Dale breaks out into various musical interludes, thus providing continuity with the existing portrayals of the merry men. The Sheriff of Nottingham, much like Alan Rickman's sheriff, is suitably camp yet menacing at different points throughout the episode. He is so power-mad that after he has conquered Nottingham with his army of robot alien knights, he will progress on to 'Lincoln…then Derby…then the world!'

In many ways, both Doctor Who and Robin Hood are similar characters. They are heroes who fight injustice in their respective times. Both are socially conservative figures, inasmuch as they do not seek to overturn society or to incite a revolution, they simply intervene where they see an injustice happening then move along. This episode received mixed reviews both from *Doctor Who* fans and mainstream TV critics. Some praised the episode for being light-hearted family fun, which is of course what *Doctor Who* essentially is supposed to be. However, some thought that it was too tongue-in-cheek, because they expected, apparently, the utmost seriousness from a series which sees a flamboyantly dressed madman ride around space and time in a blue box which is bigger on the inside. With its humour and the fact that it does not take itself too seriously, the production feels similar in tone to the series with Jonas Armstrong. However, the producers have given us a 'typical' Robin Hood, felt hat, a long bow, a fat Friar Tuck, and a large, stout Little John. The world which the producers conjured on screen is a Victorianesque merrie England of chivalry and romance. It is not a gritty or highly sexualised medieval world in the style of *Game of Thrones* or *Vikings*.

ROBIN HOOD

While the Robin Hood book had effectively died in the latter part of the twentieth century, there are a few noteworthy attempts by modern authors to present a new slant on the outlaw's story. Chief among these latter day authors is Adam Thorpe and his critically-acclaimed novel, *Hodd* (2009). In a similar manner to the framing narrative used by Walter Scott for *Ivanhoe*, the story is said to be based upon an ancient manuscript written in Latin which was found in a church after the Battle of the Somme in 1916, and which has recently been translated. The book comes complete with footnotes in order to mimic the conventions of scholarly translation, although some reviewers have argued that there are perhaps too many footnotes; moreover, the use of many Middle English words were clearly off-putting for some novel readers. Robin Hood is not the main character in the novel for it tells the biography of a monk who, in his early life was a minstrel, fell into Hodd's band. He is given the name of Muche, obviously based upon Much the Miller's son. Yet the Robin Hood of *Hodd* is not the kind of 'merrie England' outlaw that audiences are used to seeing; he is a cruel character with little to recommend him to readers.

At the time of writing, the last major cinematic portrayal of the outlaw's story was *Robin Hood* which appeared in 2010 and featured Russell Crowe in the lead role. Crowe's Robin Longstride, a middle-aged crusader, witnesses the king's death and is charged by Robert of Locksley, who has been stabbed by French mercenaries in a forest in France, to return the king's crown and sword to England. In order to do so, Longstride has to pretend to be Robin of Locksley. After John becomes king, Longstride ventures to Locksley and informs Robert's father of his son's death. As Locksley's wife, Marian, played by Cate Blanchett, cannot inherit her husband's lands, Locksley's father asks Longstride to assume Robin of Locksley's identity. He agrees to do so; he also decides to take up the cause of social justice by robbing a cart that is taking grain from the poor starving villagers to the church's granaries.

This film depicts an older Robin Hood, one who is more serious than Errol Flynn's swashbuckling and comical outlaw. There are echoes of Miller's *Royston Gower* in the Russell Crowe *Robin Hood*, as Robin becomes involved in the fight for the passage of Magna Carta; King John initially agrees to this after having heard a rousing speech from Robin Hood; besides, John also needs Robin's help to repel a French invasion, which is executed successfully. However, at the end of the movie, just as John is about to attach his seal to a 'Charter of Rights', he reneges on his pledge to the people and declares Robin Hood an outlaw. While critics had their qualms about the movie, with some rather ridiculous and unfair criticism directed towards Russell Crowe's changing accent, it is at least an attempt to historicise the Robin Hood story. The accent of the person who played Robin Hood should really not be an issue, because the only way that a film could ever be historically accurate is if its producers mastered the laws of theoretical physics, built a time machine, travelled back to the 1190s, and recorded life as it was; in any case, regarding his apparently changing 'English' accent, Crowe might have pointed to a precedent in Pierce Egan's novel which says that Robin Hood was adept at tricking people through changing his accent.

There have been no big screen portrayals of Robin Hood since the Russell Crowe movie. There was a straight-to-DVD movie entitled *Ghost of Sherwood*, in which, for some inexplicable reason, Robin sold his soul to the devil and became a zombified monster chasing Marian and Tuck through the forest. The most famous small screen Robin Hood to emerge during the 2010s, however, was based upon a relatively unknown 1950s DC comic. Robin Hood was never a big name in the world of comics and graphic novels. Yet as Allen Wright points out, there are numerous continuities in publishing methods used by printers in the 1950s and printers of broadside ballads in the 1600s: broadsides were printed on cheap paper, sold at a low price, and then numerous issues were collected together, similar to today's trade paperback graphic novels. Continuities exist also between the penny blood and comics publishing industry. With penny bloods, each issue was sold weekly and then a 'library edition' was published after their initial run. Some comics from the 1950s do see Robin meeting Wonder Woman, and there are even some graphic novels dedicated solely to retelling the Robin Hood story, such as the Classics Illustrated version of Howard Pyle's *Merry Adventures of Robin Hood* and the same company's graphic novelisation of Walter Scott's *Ivanhoe*. Even in the comic industry, superheroes based upon Robin Hood did not reach the same heights of fame as Batman or Superman. The most famous comic book character who was obviously based upon Robin Hood, however, gallivanting around in a green costume and hat while firing arrows at his enemies was Green Arrow.

Green Arrow first appeared in a short strip in *More Fun Comics* in 1941. Like his more popular counterpart, Batman, Green Arrow was a crime fighter. The true identity of the Arrow was a wealthy man named Oliver Queen. Two origin stories were published for Green Arrow, one in 1943 and an entirely different one in 1959. It is the latter which has remained part of Arrow lore to this day: Oliver Queen was stranded on an exotic island for several years; while waiting to be rescued he honed his archery talents, afterwards making his way home to save his city from criminals. There are some parallels here with one of the usual stories from the Robin Hood legend, in which Robin Hood returns from overseas to save the people of his home town from its undesirable elements. The fact that Queen is a rich man is also the equivalent of Robin Hood often being portrayed as the Earl of Huntingdon.

Green Arrow was always a minor figure in the world of comics but he entered the mainstream in 2012 when the series *Arrow* was first broadcast. The first episode does play up the Robin Hood connection, for when he returns home to Star City and takes down a corrupt businessman. He then redistributes the man's ill-gotten wealth under the name of the Hood. This is a Robin Hood for the twenty-first century who steals only from the so-called 'One Percent', a phrase found in several early episodes. This is a term that gained currency during the economic crash of 2007–08. Irresponsible lending on the subprime mortgage market in the USA led to the downfall of the investment bank, Lehman Brothers. Like a stack of dominos, other banks began to experience difficulties not only in the USA but across the world, with Northern Rock in the UK being a notable example. For some banks it was not all doom and gloom; governments in many countries decided that they were 'too big to fail' and, with tax payers' money, injected capital into them to keep them afloat. Whatever were the rights and wrongs of such measures, like an infection the 'credit crunch' spread and businesses in all sectors began to lay off workers, which in turn led to widespread unemployment. At the time, many people, particularly activists involved with the various 'Occupy' movements, noticed that the class of people who had caused the crash were still getting richer, while the rest of society had seen their wages decline. In this context calls for a 'Robin Hood Tax' from activists in America and Britain became louder. People were angry that tax payers' money was used to bail out big business and benefit the CEOs of large multinational banks, while ordinary citizens felt no benefit from it. 'The one percent' was, therefore, a pejorative term which aimed to wake people up to the fact, and *Arrow* was tapping into this discontent.

One really does get the sense, in the first season at least, that Oliver Queen is a bandit going it alone, although later it is with the help of his trusted sidekick, John Diggle (there are, of course, echoes of John Little in the name of his companion). His base is under a disused nightclub and, apart from a few electronic arrows that he has fashioned himself, his weaponry is relatively modest. The people he fights are crooks, and many of the early stories are similar to those of Batman in this respect. However, as the seasons progress, Queen finds himself having to team up with other superheroes from the DC universe such as the Flash. His lair becomes more technologically advanced and the villains become more supernatural. It is in these later series that the Green Arrow ceases to be a Robin Hood figure and becomes a superhero proper. For comic book writers, the medieval legend of Robin Hood was easily adaptable for the modern world, just as it had always been.

It is *likely* that there was a man named Robin Hood whose life and deeds, during the 1200s, gave birth to the stories that began to circulate about him. As we have seen, the most probable candidate is the Robert Hod who was found in the Yorkshire Assize records between 1225 and 1226. This man was pursued by the Sheriff of York, who in his previous employment was the Sheriff of Nottingham. Yet as we have seen, the most important thing about Robin Hood is the stories that have been successively told about him. The stories mean more than the actual life of the man himself, whoever he may have been. There is no single Robin Hood that keeps reappearing throughout history. Every new story of Robin Hood, be it the *Gest*, Munday's *Huntingdon* plays, Jonson's *Sad Shepherd*, Scott's *Ivanhoe*, or the communist *Bows Against the Barons*, Flynn's swashbuckling Robin Hood, is not an adaptation of an earlier Robin Hood story, as such, but an entirely new one. New features have been added to the Robin Hood legend over time, and these change because of a variety of factors. Each writer has attempted to make Robin Hood relevant to events in their own day. The very fact that there is no clear and identifiable Robin Hood figure from history, and there is no single authoritative text written about him, makes it clear that Robin Hood is a figure who can be endlessly reimagined. At the time of writing, a new Robin Hood movie starring Taron Egerton is in the works. It is unlikely that this will be the last portrayal of Robin Hood we will see in cinemas or on our TV screens, for the words of the early modern poet, Michael Drayton, quoted at the beginning of this book, will always hold true, and perhaps it is fitting to close with his words:

> And to the end of time the tales shall ne'er be done,
> Of Scarlock, George-a-Green, and Much the Miller's Son,
> Of Tuck, the merry friar, which many a sermon made,
> In praise of Robin Hood, the outlaws, and their trade.

Bibliography

This bibliography is a list of works which have informed my own research and it is also intended to serve as suggestions for further reading. I would encourage readers who want to keep up with the latest scholarly research in the field of Robin Hood studies to visit the website of the International Association for Robin Hood Studies. As of 2018, the Association also boasts its own open access peer-reviewed journal: *The Bulletin of the International Association for Robin Hood Studies*. The web addresses for both the Association's website and its journal are listed below.

Books, Periodicals and Manuscripts

Aberth, John, *A Knight at the Movies: Medieval History on Film* (New York: Routledge, 2003)

Addison, Joseph, *The Works of Joseph Addison*, 3 vols (New York: Harper, 1837)

——, and Richard Steele, *The Tatler*, ed. by Donald F. Bond, 3 vols (Oxford: Clarendon Press, 1987)

Ainsworth, William Harrison, Merry England; or, Nobles and Serfs, 3 vols (London: Tinsley, 1874)

——, *Windsor Castle* (London: H. Colburn, 1844)

——, *Jack Sheppard: A Romance*, 3 vols (London: Bentley, 1839)

——, *Rookwood: A Romance*, 3 vols (London: Bentley, 1834)

Andrews, Stuart, *Robert Southey: History, Politics, Religion* (Basingstoke: Palgrave, 2011)

Armours, J. F., ed., *The Original Chronicle of Andrew of Wyntoun*, 6 vols (Edinburgh and London, 1903–14)

Ashton, Owen and Stephen Roberts, *The Victorian Working-Class Writer* (London: Mansell, 1999)

Baden-Powell, Robert, *Young Knights of the Empire* (London: C. A. Pearson, 1917)

BIBLIOGRAPHY

Barczewski, Stephanie, *Myth and National Identity in Nineteenth-Century Britain: The Legends of King Arthur and Robin Hood* (Oxford: Oxford University Press, 2000)

Barton, Ann, *Ben Jonson: Dramatist* (Cambridge: Cambridge University Press, 1984)

Basdeo, Stephen, 'A Critical Edition of Little John's Answer to Robin Hood and the Duke of Lancaster', *Bulletin of the International Association for Robin Hood Studies*, 1: 1 (2018), 15-31

——, 'Robin Hood the Brute: Representations of the Outlaw in 18th-Century Criminal Biography', *Law, Crime and History*, 6: 2 (2016), 54-70

——, 'Radical Medievalism: Pierce Egan the Younger's Robin Hood, Wat Tyler, and Adam Bell', in *Imagining the Victorians*, ed. by Stephen Basdeo and Lauren Padgett, Leeds Working Papers in Victorian Studies, 15 (Leeds: LCVS), 45-64

BBC News, 2007

Blake, William, *Milton: A Poem* (London: Blake, 1804)

Blanning, Tim, *The Romantic Revolution* (London: Phoenix, 2010)

Bower, Walter *Scotichronicon*, cited in Francis J. Child, ed., *The English and Scottish Popular Ballads*, 5 vols (Boston, MA: Houghton, 1882–98)

The Boys of England, 1883

Brewer, John, *The Pleasures of the Imagination: English Culture in the Eighteenth Century*, rev. ed. (Abingdon: Routledge, 2013)

Brimblecombe, Peter 'Air Pollution and Health History', in *Air Pollution and Health*, ed. by Robert Maynard Stephen Holgate Hillel Koren Jonathan Samet Robert Maynard (Waltham: Academic Press, 2014), pp. 5-20

Burd, Alfred Henry, *Joseph Ritson: A Critical Biography* (Illinois, 1916)

Burke, Peter, *Popular Culture in Early Modern Europe*, rev. ed. (Farnham: Ashgate, 2009)

Burke, Victorian, 'Women and Early Seventeenth-Century Manuscript Culture: Four Miscellanies', *The Seventeenth Century*, 12: 2 (1997), 135-50

Butler, Marilyn, *Peacock Displayed: A Satirist in his Context* (London: Routledge, 1979)

Cadell, Robert, 'Letter to Archibald Constable 19 Nov 1819', National Library of Scotland, Edinburgh MS 323, fol. 76v.

Challinor, Jennie, 'A manuscript of Rochester's 'Upon Nothing' in a newly recovered eighteenth-century miscellany of Restoration verse', *The Seventeenth Century*, 32: 2 (2017), 161-90

Chandler, Alice, 'Sir Walter Scott and the Medieval Revival', *Nineteenth-Century Fiction*, 19: 4 (1965), 315-332

Chaucer, Chaucer, *The Canterbury Tales and Faerie Queene*, ed. by D. Laing Purves (Edinburgh: W. P. Nimmo, 1897)

Child, Francis J., ed., *The English and Scottish Popular Ballads*, ed. by Francis James Child, 5 vols (Boston, MA: Houghton, 1882–98)

Christie, Ian, *The Last Machine: Early Cinema and the Birth of the Modern World* (London: British Film Institute, 1994)

Colley, Linda, *Britons: Forging the Nation, 1707-1837* (New Haven: Yale University Press, 1992)

Coote, Lesley and Valerie Blythe Johnson, eds., *Robin Hood in Outlawed Spaces: Media, Performance, and Other New Directions* (Abingdon: Routledge, 2016)

Corrie, G. E., ed., *The Works of Hugh Latimer*, 32 vols (London: Parker Society, 1844-45)

Cox, Phillip, *Reading Adaptations: Novels and Verse Narratives on the Stage, 1790-1840* (Manchester: Manchester University Press, 2012)

Creswick, Paul, *Robin Hood and his Adventures* (London: Nister, 1917)

Daunton, Martin, 'The Wealth of the Nation', in *The Eighteenth Century*, ed. by Paul Langford (Oxford: Oxford University Press, 2002), pp. 141-82

Deloney, Mikee, 'A Review of the Year's Publications in Robin Hood Scholarship', *Bulletin of the International Association for Robin Hood Studies*, 1: 1 (2018), 32-43

Dionne, Craig and Steve Mentz, ed., *Rogues and Early Modern English Culture* (Michigan: Michigan University Press, 2004)

Dobson, R. B. and J. Taylor, eds., *Rymes of Robyn Hood: An Introduction to the English Outlaw*, rev. ed. (Stroud: Sutton, 1997)

Downes Miles, Henry, *Dick Turpin*, 4th ed. (London, 1845)

Ebert, Roger, 'Robin and Marian (1976)', https://www.rogerebert.com/reviews/robin-and-marian-1976 [Accessed 4 April 2018]

Egan, Pierce, *Robin Hood and Little John; or, the Merry Men of Sherwood Forest* (London: W. S. Johnson, 1851)

Emmett, George, Robin Hood (London: Hogarth [n. d.])

Evans, Thomas, *Old Ballads, Historical and Narrative, with Some of Modern Date, Now First Collected and Reprinted from Rare Copies with Notes*, 2 vols (London: Printed for Thomas Evans in The Strand, 1777)

Ferrall, Charles and Anna Jackson, eds., *Juvenile Literature and British Society: The Age of Adolescence, 1850-1950* (Abingdon: Routledge, 2010)

Fielding, Henry, *Jonathan Wild* (London: A. Bell, 1785)

BIBLIOGRAPHY

Fithian, E. W., *The Life of Robin Hood* (London, 1912)

Gategno, Paul de, *Ivanhoe: A Reader's Companion* (New York: Twayne Publishers, 1994)

Gent, Thomas, *The History of York* (York: [n. pub.], 1730), p. 230

Gilliatt, Edward, *In Lincoln Green: A Story of Robin Hood* (London: Seeley, 1897)

——, *Forest Outlaws; or, Saint Hugh and the King* (London: Seeley, 1887)

Gladfelder, Hal, *Criminality and Narrative in Eighteenth-Century England: Beyond the Law* (Baltimore: Johns Hopkins University Press, 2001)

Glancey, Mark, 'Warner Bros. Film Grosses, 1924-1951: The William Schaefer Ledger', *Historical Journal of Film, Radio and Television*, 15: 1 (1995), 55-74

Godwin, William, ed., *Tabart's Collection of Popular Stories for the Nursery: Newly Translated and Revised from the French, Italian, and Old English Writers*, ed. by William Godwin, 1 (London: Tabart & Co., 1809)

Grafton, Richard, 'Chronicle at Large (1569)', in *Robin Hood and Other Outlaw Tales*, ed. by Stephen Knight and Thomas Ohlgren (Kalamazoo, MI: Medieval Institute Publications, 1997), pp. 27-29

Green Arrow: A Celebration of 75 Years (Burbank, CA: DC Comics, 2016)

Green, Roger Lancelyn, *The Adventures of Robin Hood*, rev. ed. (London: Puffin, 1995)

Gribling, Barbara, *The Image of Edward the Black Prince in Georgian and Victorian England: Negotiating the Late Medieval Past* (Woodbridge: Boydell, 2017)

Griggs, Earl Leslie, *Collected Letters of Samuel Taylor Coleridge*, 6 vols (Oxford: Clarendon Press, 1956–71)

Gutch, J. M. ed., *A Lytell Geste of Robin Hode*, 2 vols (London: Longman, 1847)

Hahn, Thomas, ed., *Robin Hood in Popular Culture* (Cambridge: Brewer, 2000)

Harding, Mike, 'Robin Hood and the woodland orgies', *Guardian*, 16 April 2010, online edn, https://www.theguardian.com/travel/2010/apr/16/robin-hood-and-woodland-orgies [Accessed 23 March 2018].

Harlan-Haughey, Sarah, *The Ecology of the English Outlaw in Medieval Literature: From Fen to Greenwood* (Abingdon: Routledge, 2016)

Harris, N. ed., *The Letters of Joseph Ritson, Esq.*, 2 vols (London: William Pickering, 1833)

Hawke, Simon, *The Ivanhoe Gambit* (London: Headline, 1987)

Hawks Sterling, Sarah, *Robin Hood and his Merry Men* (London: J. Coker [n. d.])

Head, Richard, *Jackson's Recantation or, The life & death of the notorious high-way-man, now hanging in chains at Hampstead delivered to a friend a little before execution: wherein is truly discovered the whole mystery of that wicked and fatal profession of padding on the road* (London: Printed for T. B. 1674)

Hignett, Kelly, 'Co-option or criminalisation? The state, border communities and crime in early modern Europe', *Global Crime*, 9: 1-2 (2008), 35-51

Hilton, Rodney, 'The Origins of Robin Hood', *Past & Present*, No. 14 (1958), 30-44.

Holt, James C., *Robin Hood* (London: Thames and Hudson, 1982)

——, 'The Origins and Audience of the Ballads of Robin Hood', *Past & Present*, No. 18 (1960), 89-110

Hobsbawm, Eric, *Bandits*, rev. ed. (London: Abacus, 2001)

——, *Primitive Rebels*, 3rd edn (Manchester: Manchester University Press, 1971)

——, *The Age of Revolution: Europe 1789–1848* (London: Weidenfield and Nicholson, 1962)

Holmes, Richard, ed., *Defoe on Sheppard and Wild* (London: Harper, 2002)

International Association for Robin Hood Studies (IARHS): Robin Hood Scholars on the Web <http://robinhoodscholars.blogspot.co.uk/>

Ives, Edward, *A Voyage from England to India* (London: Edward and Charles Dilly, 1773)

James, G. P. R., *Forest Days* (London, 1843)

Jonson, Ben, *The Sad Shepherd; or, A Tale of Robin Hood*, ed. by Francis Waldron (London: J. Nicholls, 1783)

Kaufman, Alexander, 'Strange Genealogies: Robin Hood's Courtship with Jack Cade's Daughter and the Creation of a Fraudulent Text', in *Robin Hood in Outlawed Spaces: Media, Performance, and Other New Directions*, ed. by Leslie Coote and Valerie Blythe Johnson (Abingdon: Routledge, 2017), pp. 70-87

——, ed., *British Outlaws of Literature and History: Essays on Medieval and Early Modern Figures from Robin Hood to Twm Shon Catty* (Jefferson, NNC: MacFarland, 2011)

——, *The Historical Literature of the Jack Cade Rebellion* (Farnham: Ashgate, 2009)

——, 'John Mair's Historiographical Humanism: Portraits of Outlaws, Robbers, and Rebels in his Historia Maioris Britanniae tam Angliae quam Scotiae (History of Greater Britain)', *Enarratio*, 19 (2015), 104-18.

BIBLIOGRAPHY

——, and Shaun F. D. Hughes, and Dorsey Armstrong, eds., *Telling Tales and Crafting Books: Essays in Honor of Thomas H. Ohlgren* (Kalamazoo, Medieval Institute Publications, 2016)

Keats, John, *Lamia, Isabella, and the Eve of St Agnes* (London: Taylor & Hessey, 1820)

Keen, Maurice, *The Outlaws of Medieval Legend*, 3rd edn (Abingdon: Routledge, 2000)

Kellner, Douglas, 'The Frankfurt School and British Cultural Studies: The Missed Articulation', in *Rethinking the Frankfurt School: Alternative Legacies of Cultural Critique*, ed. by Jeffrey T. Nealon and Caren Irr (New York: State University of New York Press, 2002), pp. 31-58

Keltie, John S. ed., *The Works of Daniel Defoe* (Edinburgh: Nimmo, 1869)

Kennedy, Geoff, *Diggers, Levellers, and Agrarian Capitalism: Radical Political Thought in Seventeenth-Century England* (Lanham, MD: Lexington, 2008)

Kinney, Arthur F., ed., *Rogues, Vagabonds, and Sturdy Beggars: A New Gallery of Tudor and Stuart Rogue Literature* (Amherst, MA: University of Massachusetts Press, 1990)

Kirkpatrick, Robert J., *Children's Books History Society, Occasional Paper XI: Wild Boys in the Dock – Victorian Juvenile Literature and Juvenile Crime* (London: Children's Books History Society, 2013)

——, *From the Penny Dreadful to the Ha'Penny Dreadfuller* (London: British Library, 2012)

Knapp, Andrew and William Baldwin, *The Newgate Calendar*, 4 vols (London: J. Robins, 1824)

Knight, Stephen, 'Robin Hood and the Forest Laws', *Bulletin of the International Association for Robin Hood Studies*, 1: 1 (2018), 1-14

——, *Reading Robin Hood: Content, Form and Reception in the Outlaw Myth* (Manchester: Manchester University Press, 2015)

——, ed., *Robin Hood in Greenwood Stood: Alterity and Context in the English Outlaw Tradition* (Turnhout: Brepols, 2008)

——, ed. *Robin Hood Classic Fiction Library*, 8 vols (Abingdon: Routledge, 2005)

——, *Robin Hood: A Mythic Biography* (Ithaca: Cornell University Press, 2003)

——, ed., *Robin Hood: An Anthology of Scholarship and Criticism* (Cambridge: Brewer, 1999)

——, and Thomas Ohlgren, eds., *Robin Hood and Other Outlaw Tales* (Kalamazoo, MI: Medieval Institute Publications, 1997)

——, ed., *Robin Hood: The Forresters Manuscript, British Library Additional MS 71158* (Cambridge: Brewer, 1998)

——, *Robin Hood: A Complete Study of the English Outlaw* (Oxford: Blackwell, 1994)

La Belle Assemblée, 1820

Langford, Paul, *A Polite and Commercial People* (Oxford: Oxford University Press, 1989)

Langland, William, *Piers Plowman*, ed. by Elizabeth A. Robertson & Stephen H. A. Shepherd, Trans. E. Talbot Donaldson (New York: Norton, 2006)

Lincoln, Andrew, *Walter Scott and Modernity* (Edinburgh: Edinburgh University Press, 2007)

The Literary Chronicle and Weekly Review, 1822

Little John and Will Scarlet (London: H. Vickers, 1865), p. 183

Macfarren, George, and John Oxenford, *Robin Hood: An Opera in Three Acts* (London: Cramer, Beale and Chapel, 1860)

MacMillan's Magazine, 1866

MacNally, Leonard, *Robin Hood or Sherwood Forest. A Comic Opera.* (Dublin: J. Exshaw, 1784)

Marcellus Craig, David Marcellus, *Robert Southey and Romantic Apostasy: Political Argument in Britain, 1780-1840* (Woodbridge: Boydell, 2007)

Marston, John, *The Malcontent*, ed. by George K. Hunter, rev. ed. (Manchester: Manchester University Press, 2000)

Mass Observation, TopicCollection-17_1706.

——, TopicCollection-26_4419

——, Topic Collection-59_1413, p. 2.

——, File Report-1332_127, p. 116.

——, Marylebone, Library QQM15C, R.C.C. 8. 4. 42, Topic Collection-20_2595.

——, Bourneville Works Musical Society, Topic Collection-16_3753.

Marx, Karl and Frederich Engels, *The Communist Manifesto* (Oxford: Oxford University Press, 2008)

McCall, Andrew, *The Medieval Underworld* (London: Hamilton, 1979)

Mendez, Moses, *Robin Hood: A New Musical Entertainment. As it is Performed at the Theatre Royal in Drury Lane. The Musick Composed by the Society of the Temple of Apollo* (London: M. Cooper, 1751)

A Mery Geste of Robyn Hode and Hys Lyfe wyth a Newe Playe for to be Played in Maye Games Very Plesaunte and Full of Pastyme (London: William Copland, 1550). British Library copy, press mark C.21.C.63.

BIBLIOGRAPHY

Michelet, Jules, *The History of France*, 2 vols (New York: D. Appleton, 1847)

Miller, Thomas, *Royston Gower; or, The Days of King John* (London: J. Nichols [n. d.])

Millgate, Jane, 'Making It New: Scott, Constable, Ballantyne, and the Publication of *Ivanhoe*', *Studies in English Literature, 1500-1900* 34: 4 (1994), 795-811

Milling, Jane and Peter Thomson, eds., *The Cambridge History of British Theatre*, 3 vols (Cambridge: Cambridge University Press, 2002)

Mitchell, Rosemary, *Picturing the Past: English History in Text and Image, 1830-1870* (Oxford: Oxford University Press, 2000)

Morris, William, *A Dream of John Ball and a King's Lesson* (London: Longman, 1912)

——, and E. Belfort Bax, 'Socialism from the Root Up', *Commonweal*, 22 May 1886, p. 61

Mortimer, Mortimer, *A Time Traveller's Guide to Medieval England* (London: Vintage, 2009)

Mosley, Stephen, *The Environment in World History* (Abingdon: Routledge, 2010)

Munday, Anthony, *The Downfall of Robert, Earl of Huntington* (London: W. Leake, 1601)

——, *The Death of Robert, Earle of Huntingdon* (London: W. Leake, 1601)

Nesvet, Rebecca, 'Robert Southey, Historian of El Dorado', Keats-Shelley Journal, 61 (2012), 116-21

The Noble Birth and Gallant Atchievements of that Remarkable Out-Law Robin Hood (London: M. Haley and J. Millar, 1685)

Nollen, Scott Allen, *Robin Hood: A Cinematic History of the English Outlaw and His Scottish Counterparts* (Jefferson, NC: MacFarland, 1999)

Norbrook, David, *Poetry and Politics in the English Renaissance*, rev. ed. (Oxford: Oxford University Press, 2002)

North, Dan, 'Magic and illusion in early cinema', *Studies in French Cinema*, 1: 2 (2001), 70-79

Noyes, Alfred, *Ballads and Poems* (London: Blackwood, 1928)

O'Hayden, John, *Walter Scott: The Critical Heritage* (Abingdon: Routledge, 1970; repr. 2003)

Ohlgren, Thomas, and Lister M. Matheson, eds., *Early Rymes of Robyn Hood: An Edition of the Texts, ca. 1425 to ca. 1600* (Tempe, AZ: ACMRS, 2013)

——, *Robin Hood: The Early Poems, 1465-1560: Texts, Contexts, and Ideology* (Newark, DE: University of Delaware Press, 2007)

——, ed., *Medieval Outlaws: Ten Tales in Modern English* (Stroud: Sutton, 1998)

Olly, Mark, *The Life and Times of the Real Robyn Hoode* (Winchester: Chronos, 2015)

Peacock, Thomas Love, *Maid Marian and Crotchet Castle*, ed. by George Saintsbury (London: MacMillan, 1895)

Percy, Thomas, *Reliques of Ancient English Poetry*, ed. by E. Walford (London: F. Warne, 1880)

Perry, Ruth, 'The Famous Ballads of Anna Gordon, Mrs. Brown', in *A Cultural History of Women in the Age of Enlightenment*, ed. by Ellen Pollack, 6 vols (Michigan: Michigan State University Press, 2012)

Pitzl-Waters, Jason, 'Richard Carpenter (obit.)', *Patheos*, 3 March 2012, online edn, http://www.patheos.com [Accessed 20 March 2017]

Phillips, Helen, ed., *Bandit Territories: British Outlaws and Their Traditions* (Cardiff: University of Wales Press, 2008)

——, ed., *Robin Hood: Medieval and Post-Medieval* (Dublin: Four Courts, 2005)

Planché, J. R., *Maid Marian; or, The Huntress of Arlingford* (London, 1822)

A Pleasant Conceyted Comedie of George a Greene, the Pinner of Wakefield (London: Simon Stafford, 1599)

Pollack, Ellen, ed., *A Cultural History of Women in the Age of Enlightenment*, 6 vols (Michigan: Michigan State University Press, 2012)

Pollard, A. J., *Imagining Robin Hood: The Late Medieval Stories in Historical Context* (Abingdon: Routledge, 2007)

Pope, Harrison G., Jr. et al., 'Evolving Ideals of Male Body Image as Seen Through Action Toys', *International Journal of Eating Disorders*, 26: 1 (1999), 65-72

Potter, Lois and Joshua Calhoun, eds., *Images of Robin Hood: Medieval to Modern* (Newark, DE: University of Delaware Press, 2008)

Power, M. J., 'London and the Control of the 'Crisis' of the 1590s', *History*, 70: 230 (1985), 371-85 (p. 371).

Pratt, Lynda, ed., *Robert Southey and the Contexts of English Romanticism* (Aldershot: Ashgate, 2006)

Pyle, Howard, *The Merry Adventures of Robin Hood* (New York, 1883; repr. New York: Charles Scribner, 1927)

Quiller-Couch, Arthur, *The Oxford Book of Ballads* (Oxford: Oxford University Press, 1920)

Raimond, Jean, 'Southey's Early Writings and the Revolution', *Yearbook of English Studies*, 19 (1989), 181-96

BIBLIOGRAPHY

Ramey, Lynn and Tison Pugh, eds., *Filming the Other Middle Ages: Race, Class, and Gender in Medieval Cinema* (Basingstoke: Palgrave, 2007)

Reynolds, J. H., 'Sonnets on Robin Hood', in *A Lytell Geste of Robin Hode with Other Ancient and Modern Ballads and Songs Relating to this Celebrated Yeoman to which is Prefixed his History and Character Grounded Upon Other Documents than those Made Use of by Mister Ritson*, ed. by John Mathew Gutch, 2 Vols (London: Longman, 1847), 2: 426-27

Reynolds, G. W. M., *The Mysteries of London*, 2 vols (London: G. Vickers, 1846)

Reynolds's Newspaper, 1869

Ritson, Joseph, ed., *Robin Hood: A Collection of All the Ancient Poems, Songs, and Ballads*, 2 vols (London: T. Egerton, 1795)

Robin Hood: A Tale of the Olden Time, 2 vols (Edinburgh: Oliver and Boyd, 1819)

Robin Hood and His Crew of Souldiers (London: J. Davis, 1661)

Robin Hood: An Opera (London: J. Watts, 1730)

Santini, Monica, *The Impetus of Amateur Scholarship: Discussing and Editing Medieval Romances in Late-Eighteenth and Nineteenth-Century Britain* (Bern: Peter Lang, 2009)

Sartore, Melissa, *Outlawry, Governance, and Law in Medieval England* (New York: Peter Lang, 2013)

Scott, Walter, *The Complete Poetical Works* (London: H. Frowde, 1904)

——, *Ivanhoe: A Romance*, 3 vols (Edinburgh: Ballantyne, 1820)

——, *Rob Roy*, 3 vols (Edinburgh: Ballantyne, 1818)

——, *The Antiquary*, 3 vols (Edinburgh: Ballantyne, 1816)

Shakespeare, William, *The Complete Plays*, 8 vols (London: Folio Society, 1997)

Simeone, W. E., 'The Robin Hood of Ivanhoe', *The Journal of American Folklore*, 74: 293 (1961), 230-234

Singman, J. L., *Robin Hood: The Shaping of a Legend* (Westport, CT: Greenwood, 1998)Smith, Alexander, *A Complete History of the Lives and Robberies of the Most Notorious Highwaymen*, ed. by Arthur Heyward (London: Routledge, 1927)

Southey, Charles Cuthbert, ed., *The Life and Correspondence of Robert Southey* (New York, 1855)

Southey, Robert, *Robin Hood: A Fragment* (Edinburgh: Blackwood, 1847)

——, *The Poetical Works* (Paris: A. & W. Galignani, 1829)

——, *Wat Tyler* (London: W. Hone, 1817)

——, 'Harold; or, the Castle of Morford (1791)', Bodleian MS. Eng. Misc. e. 21.

Spraggs, Gillian, *Outlaws and Highwaymen: The Cult of the Robber in England from the Middle Ages to the Nineteenth Century* (London: Pimlico, 2001)

Spring, Joel, *Images of American Life: A History of Ideological Management in Schools, Movies, Radio and Television* (New York: State University of New York, 1992)

Springhall, John, 'Pernicious Reading? The Penny Dreadful as Scapegoat for Late-Victorian Juvenile Crime', *Victorian Periodicals Review*, 27: 4 (1994), 326-49

Stevenson, R. L., *The Black Arrow* (London: Cassell, 1916)

Stocqueler, J. H., *Maid Marian the Forest Queen* (London, 1849)

Suzuki, Mihoko, 'The London Apprentice Riots of the 1590s and the Fiction of Thomas Deloney', *Criticism*, 38: 2 (1996), 181-217

Tennyson, Alfred, *The Foresters: Robin Hood and Maid Marian* (London: MacMillan, 1895)

Thierry, M. A., *The History of the Conquest of England by the Normans*, Trans. William Hazlitt, 2 vols (London: Bogue, 1847).

Thoms, William, ed., *Early English Prose Romances*, ed. by William Thomas, 3 vols (London: W. Pickering, 1828)

Thorsheim, Peter, *Inventing Pollution: Coal, Smoke, and Culture in Britain since 1800* (Ohio: Ohio University Press, 2009)

Timbs, John, *The Romance of London: Strange Stories, Scenes, and Remarkable Persons of the Great Town* (London: Frederick Warne & Co., 1865)

The Times, 1861

Trease, Geoffrey, 'Sixty years on', *Children's Literature in Education*, 27: 3 (1996), 131–141

——, *Bows Against the Barons*, 5th ed. (London: Hodder and Stoughton, 1979)

Troost, Linda V., 'Robin Hood Musicals in Eighteenth-Century London', in *Robin Hood in Popular Culture*, ed. by Thomas Hahn (Cambridge: D. S. Brewer, 2000)

Truesdale, Mark, *The King and Commoner Tradition: Carnivalesque Politics in Medieval and Early Modern Literature* (Abingdon: Routledge, 2018)

United Empire (London: Royal Empire Society, 1947)

The Universal Magazine of Knowledge and Pleasure, 1760

Valentine-Harris, P. 'Who was Robin Hood?' *Folklore*, 66: 4 (1955), 413-15

——, *The Truth About Robin Hood* (Mansfield, 1951)

Walter, Henry, *A History of England*, 7 vols (London: Rivington, 1828)

Wiles, David, *The Early Plays of Robin Hood* (Cambridge: Brewer, 1981)

Williams, Williams, 'The Adventures of Robin Hood', *The Picturegoer*, 8: 393 (1938), 86-96

Winstanley, John, *Poems Written Occasionally, Interspersed with Many Others by Several Ingenious Hands* (London, 1742)

Wordsworth, William, *The Complete Poetical Works* (London: Macmillan, 1888)

——, *The Prelude, Or, Growth of a Poet's Mind: An Autobiographical Poem* (London: E. Moxon, 1850)

Wright, Allen, "Begone knave! Robbery is out of fashion hereabouts': Robin Hood and the Comics Code', in *Bandit Territories: British Outlaws and their Traditions*, ed. by Helen Phillips (Cardiff: University of Wales Press, 2008), pp. 217-32

Websites and Databases

Basdeo, Stephen, *Here begynneth a lytell geste of Robyn Hode*, www.gesteofrobinhood.com

Bodleian Library Broadside Ballads, http://ballads.bodleian.ox.ac.uk/

British Fiction, 1800–1829: A Database of Production, Circulation, and Reception, Centre for Editorial and Intertextual Research, Cardiff University, http://www.british-fiction.cf.ac.uk/index.html

Bulletin of the International Association for Robin Hood Studies, https://bulletin.iarhs.org/index.php/IARHSBulletin/index

English Poetry, 1579–1830: Spenser and the Tradition, http://spenserians.cath.vt.edu

Knight, Stephen and Thomas Ohlgren, ed., *Robin Hood and Other Outlaw Tales*, http://d.lib.rochester.edu/teams/text/robin-hood-and-the-curtal-friar

Mass Observation, www.massobservation.amdigital.co.uk

Old Bailey Online, https://www.oldbaileyonline.org

Oxford Dictionary of National Biography, www.odnb.com

Robert Louis Stevenson Club, http://robert-louis-stevenson.org/robert-louis-stevensons-library/

Romantic Circles, https://www.rc.umd.edu/

Spraggs, Gillian, *Outlaws and Highwaymen*, www.outlawsandhighwaymen. com
Wright, Allen, *Robin Hood: Bold Outlaw*, https://boldoutlaw.com
UCSB, *English Broadside Ballad Archive*, https://ebba.english.ucsb.edu/

Audio and Visual Media

The Adventures of Robin Hood, dir. Michael Curtiz and William Keighley (Warner Bros., 1938)
The Adventures of Robin Hood, Produced by Hannah Weinstein (Sapphire Films, 1955–59)
Arrow, Produced by Greg Berlanti, Marc Guggenheim and Andrew Kreisberg (The CW, 2012–)
The Arrows of Robin Hood, dir. Sergei Tarasov (Riga Film Studio, 1975)
The Ballad of the Valiant Knight, Ivanhoe, dir. Sergei Tarasov (MosFilm, 1983)
Dick Turpin, Produced by Richard Carpenter (ITV, 1979–82)
Ivanhoe, dir. Douglas Camfield (ITV and CBS, 1982)
Ivanhoe, dir. Herbert Brennon (Universal, 1913)
Ivanhoe, dir. Leedham Bantock (1913)
The Legend of Robin Hood, dir. Eric Davidson (BBC, 1975)
Maclise, Daniel, *Robin Hood and His Merry Men Entertaining Richard the Lionheart in Sherwood Forest*, 1839. Oil on canvas. Nottingham City Museums and Galleries
Maid Marian and her Merry Men, Produced by Tony Robinson (BBC, 1989–94)
The New Adventures of Robin Hood, Produced by Tom Kuhn (Turner, 1997–98)
Princess of Thieves, dir. Peter Hewitt (Disney, 1991)
Robin and Marian, dir. Richard Lester (Columbia, 1976)
Robin Hood, dir. Ridley Scott (Universal, 2010)
Robin Hood, Produced by Dominic Minghella and Foz Allen (BBC, 2006–09)
Robin Hood, dir. John Irving (Working Title, 1991)
Robin Hood, dir. Wolfgang Reitherman (Disney, 1973)
Robin Hood, dir. Alan Dwan (United Artists, 1922)
Robin Hood (American Éclair, 1912)
Robin Hood (British and Colonial Film Company, 1912)

BIBLIOGRAPHY

Robin Hood and his Merry Men, dir. Percy Stowe (Clarendon Film Co., 1908)

Robin Hood: Men in Tights, dir. Mel Brookes (Columbia TriStar, 1993)

Robin of Sherwood, Produced by Richard Carpenter (Goldcrest, 1984–86)

Robin Hood: Prince of Thieves, dir. Kevin Reynolds (Morgan Creek, 1991)

Robin Hood: Prince of Thieves OST (Warner Bros., 1991)

Rocket Robin Hood, Produced by Al Guest (Trillium Productions, 1966)

Star Trek: The Next Generation, dir. Cliff Bole (Paramount Domestic Television, 1987–94)

The Story of Robin Hood and his Merrie Men, Ken Annakin (Disney, 1952)

Windus, William, *The Outlaw*, 1861. Oil on canvas. Manchester: Manchester Art Gallery

Wolfshead: The Legend of Robin Hood, dir. John Houghton (Hammer, 1969)

Index

INDEX

INDEX

INDEX